VOICES OF HISTORY
Speeches that Changed the World

▼

SIMON SEBAG MONTEFIORE

WEIDENFELD & NICOLSON

First published in Great Britain in 2019 by Weidenfeld & Nicolson
First published in paperback in 2020 by Weidenfeld & Nicolson,
an imprint of The Orion Publishing Group Ltd
Carmelite House, 50 Victoria Embankment
London EC4Y 0DZ

An Hachette UK Company

1 3 5 7 9 10 8 6 4 2

A CIP catalogue record for this book
is available from the British Library.

ISBN (Paperback) 978-1-4746-0993-7
ISBN (eBook) 978-1-4746-0994-4

Typeset by Input Data Services Ltd, Somerset

Printed and bound in Great Britain by Clays Ltd, Elcograf S.p.A.

MIX
Paper from
responsible sources
FSC® C104740

www.weidenfeldandnicolson.co.uk
www.orionbooks.co.uk

To my darling son Sasha

Contents

Introduction   xv
Acknowledgements   xxvii
Author's Note   xxviii

Resistance

Boudicca, 'This is a woman's resolve', AD 61   3
Elizabeth I, 'The heart and stomach of a king', 8 August 1588   5
John Boyega, 'Black lives have always mattered', 3 June 2020   7
Eleazar Ben Yair, 'Let us die before we become slaves', AD 73   10
Winston Churchill, 'Blood, toil, tears and sweat',
     13 May 1940   15
Emmeline Pankhurst, 'I am here as a soldier', 13 November 1913   18

Dreamers

Martin Luther King, Jr, 'I have a dream', 28 August 1963   23
Sojourner Truth, 'Ain't I a woman?', 1863 version   28
Muhammad Ali, 'Wait till you see Muhammad Ali',
     30 October 1974   32
Michelle Obama, 'Be the very best that you can be',
     2 April 2009   34

Freedom

Simón Bolívar, 'We are not Europeans; we are not Indians;
     we are but a mixed species', 15 February 1819   41
Toussaint Louverture, 'I want liberty and equality to reign',
     29 August 1793   43
Jawaharlal Nehru, 'At the stroke of the midnight hour',
     14 August 1947   44

Nelson Mandela, 'Rainbow nation', 10 May 1994   46
Winston Churchill, 'We shall fight on the beaches',
    4 June 1940   49

Rise and Fall

Muawiyah, 'When they pull, I loosen', 7th century AD   53
Elizabeth I, 'I have reigned with your loves',
    30 November 1601   54
Winston Churchill, 'This was their finest hour', 18 June 1940   56
Barack Obama, 'America is a place where all things are
    possible', 4 November 2008   58

Decency

Abraham Lincoln, 'Until every drop of blood drawn by the
    lash shall be paid by another drawn with the sword',
    4 March 1865   63
John F. Kennedy, 'Ask not what your country can do for you',
    20 January 1961   66
Chimamanda Ngozi Adichie, 'The ability of human beings
    to make and remake themselves for the better',
    December 2012   70
Malala Yousafzai, 'One pen and one book can change the
    world', 12 July 2013   73
Mohandas Gandhi, 'I have faith in the righteousness of our
    cause', 11 March 1930   76
Susan B. Anthony, 'Are women persons?', February–June 1873   79
Elizabeth II, 'We will be with our friends; we will be with our
    families; we will meet again', 5 April 2020   82

Battlefields

George S. Patton, Jr, 'I am personally going to shoot that
    paper-hanging sonofabitch Hitler', 5 June 1944   87
Alexander the Great, 'You have Alexander', November 333 BC   89
George W. Bush, 'Today, our nation saw evil',
    11 September 2001   91

Tim Collins, 'Tread lightly there', 19 March 2003   95
Franklin D. Roosevelt, 'A date which will live in infamy',
      8 December 1941   97

Defiance

Cleopatra, 'I will not be triumphed over', 30 BC   103
Oliver Cromwell, 'In the name of God, go!', 20 April 1653   105
Ronald Reagan, 'Mr Gorbachev, tear down this wall!',
      12 June 1987   107
Winston Churchill, 'The Few', 20 August 1940   110

Terror

Al-Hajjaj ibn Yusuf, 'By God I'll grind you down to dust', Kufa,
      Iraq, AD 694   113
Nikolai Yezhov, Josef Stalin and others, 'These swine must be
      strangled', 4 December 1936   114
Abu Bakr al-Baghdadi, 'Declare the Caliphate', 29 June 2014   118
Genghis Khan, 'The greatest pleasure', 13th century   120
Osama bin Laden, 'America is struck', 7 October 2001   121
Maximilien Robespierre, 'Virtue and terror', 5 February 1794   124

Trials

Socrates, 'The unexamined life is not worth living', 399 BC   131
Nikolai Yezhov, 'Shoot me quietly', 3 February 1940   136

Follies

Richard Nixon, 'No whitewash at the White House',
      30 April 1973   141
Neville Chamberlain, 'Peace for our time', 30 September 1938   144
Adolf Hitler, 'I am at the head of the strongest army in the
      world', 11 December 1941   145

Power

Theodora, 'Imperial purple is the noblest burial sheet', AD 532   153
Josef Stalin, 'We need new blood', 16 October 1952   154
Abraham Lincoln, 'Government of the people, by the people,
      for the people', 19 November 1863   158
Donald Trump, 'Make America great again', 16 June 2015   159
Aung San Suu Kyi, 'It is not power that corrupts, but fear',
      July 1991   165
Xi Jinping, 'History is our best teacher', 14 May 2017   168

Peacemakers

Anwar al-Sadat, 'I have come to Jerusalem, as the City of
      Peace', 20 November 1977   173
Yitzhak Rabin, 'Enough of blood and tears', 13 September 1993   177

Revolution

Georges Danton, 'Dare, dare again, always dare!',
      2 September 1792   183
Mao Zedong, 'The Chinese people have stood up!',
      21 September 1949   185
Vladimir Ilyich Lenin, 'Power to the Soviets', September 1917   187
Ruhollah Khomeini, 'I shall smash this government in the
      teeth', February 1979   189

Warmongers

Urban II, 'Enter upon the road to the Holy Sepulchre',
      27 November 1095   193
Cato the Elder, 'Carthage must be destroyed!', 149 BC   196

Genocide

Adolf Hitler, 'The annihilation of the Jewish race in Europe',
      30 January 1939   199
Heinrich Himmler, 'The Jewish people are going to be
      exterminated', 4 October 1943   201

Good vs Evil

Elie Wiesel, 'The perils of indifference', 12 April 1999   207
Boris Yeltsin, 'We are all guilty', 18 July 1998   212
Chaim Herzog, 'Hate, ignorance and evil', 10 November 1975   214

Prophets

Moses, 'Thou shall not kill', Exodus 20, Verses 1–26   219
Jesus of Nazareth, 'Blessed are the poor in spirit', Sermon on the
    Mount, St Matthew's Gospel, 1st century AD   221
The Prophet Mohammed, 'Turn then your face towards the
    Sacred Mosque', from the Surah al-Baqarah ('The Cow'),
    Verse 2 (144–50), 7th century AD   223

Warnings

J. Robert Oppenheimer, 'We are not only scientists; we are
    men, too', 2 November 1945   227
Greta Thunberg, 'We can't solve a crisis without treating it
    as a crisis', 3 December 2018   229

Goodbyes

Eva Perón, 'Remain faithful to Perón', 17 October 1951   233
Martin Luther King, Jr, 'I've seen the promised land',
    3 April 1968   237
Attila the Hun, funeral address by his henchman, 'Lord of the
    bravest tribes fell neither by enemy's blows nor treachery
    but by rejoicing', AD 53   240
Richard Nixon, 'Nobody will ever write a book about my
    mother', 9 August 1974   241
William Pitt the Younger, 'Europe is not to be saved by any
    single man', 9 November 1805   245
Nero, 'What an artist the world is losing in me', 9 June 68 AD   246
Barack Obama, 'We do these things because of who we are',
    1 May 2011   249

Napoleon Bonaparte, 'Soldiers of my Old Guard: I bid you
    farewell', 20 April 1814   253
Edward VIII, 'The woman I love', 11 December 1936   255
Alexander the Great, 'Depart!', August 324 BC   257
Charles I, 'I go from a corruptible to an incorruptible
    crown', 30 January 1649   262
Ronald Reagan, 'Nothing ends here; our hopes and our
    journeys continue', 28 January 1986   266

Introduction

Friends! Brothers and sisters! Comrades! Fellow citizens! Your
majesties and highnesses! My countrymen! My children! Fellow
soldiers! Ladies and gentlemen!

You can tell much by the opening of a speech. Elizabeth I
begins hers majestically, 'My loving people'. Mandela says,
'Comrades and friends'. Lincoln starts: 'Fellow countrymen'.
Toussaint Louverture combines 'Brothers and friends!'. For
Robespierre: 'Citizen-representatives of the people'. Michelle
Obama calls her audience of schoolgirls 'future leaders of the
world'. Stalin changes his entire relationship with the Soviet
peoples when, after the Nazi invasion, he addresses them on 3
July 1941 not just as Communist 'comrades' but as 'brothers and
sisters, I am addressing you, dear friends'. Eleazar, Jewish rebel
leader, calls his people 'generous friends' when he asks them to
commit mass suicide with him. Calling an audience 'friends' is
often a good start, though Cromwell, talking to English Parliamentarians, takes a different approach: 'Ye pack of mercenary
wretches. . . . Ye sordid prostitutes'. Donald Trump does not
address his audience directly but just says: 'Wow! Whoa! That's
some group of people. Thousands!' The opening is all about
defining the relationship – the terms of the contract, contact
and compact – between speaker and audience. Invite them in,
make them comfortable, but not necessarily too comfortable,
because even the most egalitarian speaker must hold the helm
and set the course.

This is a wholly new book of the greatest speeches – and
a companion to my *Written in History: Letters that Changed the
World*. These are speeches everyone should know. Some are

familiar and rightly so; some, I hope, are new to you.

I would like to tell you the speeches that changed the world were the most poetic, truthful and decent; hymns of liberty, paeans of tolerance. Yes, there are many of those here, but the most powerful speeches are not all about love, beauty and poetry – they are often atrocious projections of naked power, of lies, hatred and calumny, dehumanising so-called 'enemies' with cruel hyperbole. Such speeches move worlds just as much as those of the noblest spirit and heroic courage. This collection includes the best and worst. Some of the most diabolical are here, partly for the fascination of seeing words that convinced so many in other epochs to do unspeakable things, partly to wonder at their obvious combination of evil and absurdity. Above all, I include these wicked speeches because in our own times, the very truth of these events has been challenged in an age of historical ignorance, resurgent hatreds and conspiracy theories. It has never been more important to see and hear the evidence, more essential to know such things, and realise there were times when mere words helped make violence and hatred not just normal and acceptable but desirable.

Many of these speeches are viscerally relevant today even though they were delivered centuries ago: in the age of populism, when widespread indignation and exasperation with traditional parliaments and professional politicians is fierce, Cromwell's furious attack on his own parliamentarians sounds familiar to us – he felt he was 'draining the swamp'. It is impossible to listen to the speeches of Sojourner Truth, Martin Luther King and Toussaint Louverture without reflecting on how racism, in America and Europe, has survived and thrived. John Boyega's passionate address just after the murder of George Floyd in America, the killing that launched an international campaign against racism, catches the righteous fury of the Black Lives Matter movement of 2020. It is tragic that in the twenty-first century it is relevant to include a speech against antisemitism – anti-Jewish racism – and anti-Zionism by Chaim Herzog. In Stalin's speech, we hear the original Stalinist version of the antisemitism now resurgent on the American and British 'progressive' Left. Reading these speeches, we need to remember the idea attributed to Edmund Burke but originally spoken by John Stuart Mill during a speech in 1867: 'Bad men need nothing more to compass their ends than that good men should look on and do nothing.'

The best of these speeches are examples of human decency and sublime literature that can be enjoyed on every level. The finest are a marriage of speaker, message, audience and time, a mix of skill, felicity, serendipity and synchronicity that together, through a form of personal alchemy, can make gold. It is easy to make rules on the best oratory. It must be short without glibness; substantial without ennui; powerful without haughtiness; dramatic without contrivance; confident without bombast; intimate without condescension; emotional without melodrama; courageous without bravado; beautiful without artifice; passionate without posturing; poignant without plangency; honest without vanity; world-historical without grandiloquence. 'In an orator, the acuteness of the logicians, the wisdom of the philosophers, the language almost of poetry, the memory of lawyers, the voice of tragedians, the gesture almost of the best actors, is required,' wrote Cicero, one of the Rome's best speakers, in his essay *On Oratory*. 'Nothing therefore is more rarely found among mankind than a consummate orator.' It was written in 55 BC but is just as true today.

The most revealing speeches are those that are the most personal: in Alexander the Great's speeches, we can hear across two millennia his pride in his own divine greatness – and fury at the ingratitude and impertinence of his mutinous men. Nixon's farewell to his staff must be the most awkward speech of his life. In Stalin's secret last speech, we are witnessing the real tyrant as vicious old man.

Authenticity and brevity. The essence of a great speech is always the ability to communicate a simple message crafted to suit the chosen audience, not only through words but through the fusion of the character of the speaker and the message itself. The authenticity of that matching of speaker and message decides its success or failure. It's this that makes Elizabeth II's COVID-19 speech so effective.

Oratory is theatrical. It requires some of the gifts of the thespian and the tricks of the showman but it is very different. At the theatre, the audience knows the actor is playing an imaginary part and wishes to enter into the fantasy. In oratory, it is the opposite. There is indeed a stage, a show, a drama, but while knowing this is a performance, the audience must trust that the 'actor' is not acting at all, must believe in his or her sincerity and recognise their total self-belief. 'The eloquent man is he who is no beautiful speaker but who is desperately drunk with a certain belief,' noted Ralph Waldo Emerson. That self-belief, abnormal in most mortals, essential in leaders, can be both virtue and sickness: the asset of confidence can so easily degenerate into psychopathic narcissism.

'All great speakers were bad speakers at first,' argued Emerson. This is not always true: Danton was a born speaker – you can hear his passionate energy. Compare Hitler and Churchill. Both worked exceedingly hard on their speeches. Photographs of Hitler by his court photographer show him posing like a camp actor as he worked on his stage show. His henchman Goebbels recalled that he rewrote each speech about five times, dictating changes to three secretaries simultaneously. Churchill, who started with a slight stammer and a lisp, proves Emerson's point. He wrote his speeches by hand, over and over again, correcting and polishing. Hitler's performances were theatrical spectaculars of physical athleticism, sometimes lasting hours, delivered to crowds first in sweaty beer halls then in illuminated stadiums. Yet on paper, his phrases seem mediocre. Churchill's were the opposite, delivered stolidly in House of Commons or BBC studio, but the phrases are golden and timeless. Both worked well on radio: would either have worked on television? Certainly not Churchill. Yet the melodrama of the movie *Triumph of the Will* shows that Hitler might have shone if CNN had existed to broadcast his long rallies.

In some ways, the speaker is extraordinarily exposed but the payoff is the ability to communicate directly to the audience. The speeches of the French Revolution often ended with the arrest and beheading of the speaker – a spontaneity that Robespierre and Danton both encouraged, both fell victim to. It was the same in the assembly of democratic Athens. Alexander the Great could have been cut down by his mutinous soldiers when he addressed them so rudely. The speaker is taking a risk, and that very gamble can win the love of the audience: Napoleon's speech to his Old Guard appeals to the intimacy of general and soldier. When he returned to seize power for the Hundred Days, he only had to speak to them and they defected to him.

In 1989, the Romanian dictator Nikolai Ceauşescu lost control of his country in a speech that culminated in booing then revolution. He fled by helicopter and was then arrested and executed. In twenty-first-century Venezuela, the brutal bungling dictator Nicolás Maduro regularly revealed his coarseness with comical mispronunciations: during a speech on education, he meant to quote Jesus multiplying the 'loaves and the fishes', but instead said, 'to multiply ourselves like Christ multiplied the penises – sorry the fish and the bread', to national guffaws. The Spanish words for fish and penis are similar – but not identical.

The length of a speech is often proportional to its vainglory. 'Brevity is the great charm of eloquence,' decreed Cicero, who believed 'the best orator is to the point and impassioned.' While Lincoln's masterpiece at Gettysburg is just 278 words long, Fidel Castro, Communist dictator of Cuba, once spoke for seven hours: the image he was seeking was machismo personified;

virile, almost priapic, endurance coupled with dictatorial omnipotence. The wartime speeches of Hitler and Italian dictator Mussolini were also preposterously long. 'Speeches measured by the hour,' said Jefferson, 'die with the hour.' Pitt the Younger's speech lasted a few seconds but is sublime. The power to bore an audience is a classic manifestation of tyranny. The freer an audience the less it will tolerate.

Yet fairground hucksterism not only works – it is often mesmerising. As Hitler, Eva Perón and others in this collection show, audiences revel in the brazenness of charisma, bombast and melodrama: bold theatricality and the excitement of crowd behaviour can combine to enchant and intoxicate, audiences embracing a sort of frenzied madness.

There is a difference between demagoguery and oratory: 'Eloquence cannot exist under a despotic form of government,' wrote Tacitus in his essay *The Corruption of Eloquence*. 'It can only exist in lands where free institutions flourish. There is nothing in the world like a persuasive speech to fuddle the mental apparatus and upset the convictions and debauch the emotions of an audience not practised in the tricks and delusions of oratory.' But the difference between vulgarity and eloquence is in the eye of the beholder.

Worthy virtue can bore its listeners to death: 'In doing good, we are generally cold, and languid, and sluggish; and of all things afraid of being too much in the right,' comments Edmund Burke. 'But the works of malice and injustice are quite in another style. They are finished with a bold, masterly hand; touched as they are with the spirit of those vehement passions that call forth all our energies, whenever we oppress and persecute.' The Devil often has the best lines. Robespierre's call for Terror is powerful, elegant and bloodthirsty. But not always. Himmler is no orator.

Speeches are tools of power as essential as artillery or gold: 'instruments that a president uses to govern', in the words of

JFK's speechwriter Ted Sorenson. Even without the poetry of a Martin Luther King, there are methods to make them work. 'If you have an important point to make,' said Churchill, 'don't try to be subtle and clever, use a piledriver. Make that point one time, hit it again. A third time. A tremendous whack!'

Each speech tells a story in which hindsight can be heartbreaking. Egyptian president Sadat and Israeli prime minister Rabin both had made their careers as warlords – and when they made peace, their speeches were powerful, not just because they were superbly written (Rabin's especially touching since he was in person shy, rough and reticent). They are even more poignant now that we know that both of them paid for their courage with their lives. It is impossible to read Martin Luther King's 'I've seen the Promised Land' without feeling that he understood that he was doomed.

Then we have the ritual of the last goodbye. The dying Evita's adieu from the Casa Rosada is every bit as emotional as the song from the musical she inspired. Napoleon's tearful departure verges on cheap melodrama – very different from the sad elegiac haughtiness of Charles I before his execution. It is hard to grieve for the merciless secret police killer Yezhov who appeals to his master Stalin before he is shot.

The best speakers have the ability to make ideas and aspirations come alive – 'thoughts on fire', as William Jenning Bryan, the American populist, put it – so that their audiences feel they are part of something greater than themselves, part of a dream that may come true. JFK's inaugural speech and Martin Luther King's 'I have a dream' both achieve this.

Wartime speeches have special functions: they depend on the management of expectations. Elizabeth I made a virtue of the perceived weakness of femininity. Churchill 'mobilised the English language and sent it into battle' (in the words of CBS reporter Edward Murrow and reused by JFK) by offering only blood and tears. The Jewish commander Eleazar at Masada persuaded 900 men, women and children that they should commit suicide en masse rather than face execution, slavery and rape at the hands of the Roman victors.

Speeches that begin wars offer easy prizes in return for little blood spilled – and that blood hopefully foreign. Pope Urban II invented Christian holy war as the equivalent of Islamic jihad and inspired the first crusaders to take Jerusalem, offering a mix of faith, penance and plunder. Hitler's speech opening the Second World War with his invasion of Poland is full of militaristic bravado. His audience believed victory was assured since he had outwitted all the great world powers and annexed two countries without a shot fired. Similarly, when he declared war on America in December 1941, he believed he was losing nothing and intimidating America to keep out of Europe. The consequences were the opposite of those intended.

Elizabeth, Hitler, Churchill, Lincoln wrote their own speeches, but JFK worked on his with Sorenson; Reagan's were brilliantly written by Peggy Noonan. The best speech writers are literary ventriloquists. They are *moulded* to the speaker but they can also *invent* a new persona. Noonan's cowboy's lament for Reagan's retirement evokes the myth of an old cowboy of the American West:

> There's still a lot of brush to clear out at the ranch, fences that need repair and horses to ride. But I want you to know that if the fires ever dim, I'll leave my phone and address behind just in case you need a foot soldier. Just let me know and I'll be there, as long as words don't leave me and as long as this sweet country strives to be special during its shining moment on earth.

But it must be plausible to maintain authenticity. Slickness can be suspicious; loquacity so quickly becomes verbosity. Trotsky was the wizard of oratory during the Russian Revolution, but ultimately the rough Bolsheviks distrusted his showmanship, preferring a speaker who made a virtue out of his own lack of magic which he presented as plain-speaking: Stalin. Gladstone's performances to huge audiences were astonishing for their sanctimonious energy but they were also displays of grandiloquent vanity pricked by his witty rival Disraeli, who called Gladstone 'a sophisticated rhetorician, inebriated with the exuberance of his own verbosity'.

The nature of speeches has changed over history thanks to technology. Some of the speeches from the ancient world were recorded by historians who wholly or partly invented speeches they had not heard – but it is likely that Josephus, Tacitus and others quoted here did talk to those who were present. Some of these speeches were the regular table talk of a monarch given to tiny groups of courtiers, such as Genghis Khan's reflections on conquest and Muawiyah's on the art of ruling. Cleopatra's line about her fate was probably repeated by Octavian and recorded by the well-connected historian Livy – I count it as a speech because she was aware they were perhaps her last words on history's stage.

Nero's entire life as emperor was a self-conscious theatrical performance – as if he was living on a Roman reality TV show. If he had been alive today, he would certainly have starred in one. Of all the tyrants of the ancient world, he is strangely the most modern. He would have fitted well into the brutal buffoonery of twenty-first-century politics.

For most of human history, speeches could only be heard by a small number of people, thousands, not more. Those given in the Roman Senate, the Athenian Ecclesia or the English Parliament were initially heard only by those present. It was the same with the battlefield speeches of Alexander the Great before Issus or Henry V before Agincourt. The problem was solved on battlefields by the officers repeating the speeches to their regiments. In the age of printing, the public could read an official version – Elizabeth I's Tilbury speech was published. Before TV or radio, political speeches were a form of entertainment, almost as much as theatre or musical recital. Thousands turned up to hear Gladstone's Midlothian Campaign.

The invention of the microphone in 1877 meant that by the early years of the twentieth century, speakers could address much larger crowds, leading to stadium spectaculars: 'I know that men are won over less by the written than by the spoken word, that every great movement on this earth owes its growth to great orators and not to great writers,' Hitler wrote in *Mein Kampf*. But live harangues to large crowds lacked the intimacy that the new technologies of TV delivered in the 1950s.

Television favoured some, undermined others. Kennedy looked glamorous, Nixon furtive. Speakers could reach an even larger audience yet attention spans grew shorter. Some speeches were reduced to just the phrases – 'the soundbite'. Tape recordings and video also meant that speeches could be given in private then copied and broadcast. The Iranian Revolution was won not on the streets or the *minbars* but in cassettes smuggled into the country bearing the speeches of Khomeini; Osama bin Laden spread his jihadism through smuggled videotapes.

The internet and the podcast restored interest in listening to words, yet one might have expected twenty-four-hour news, multi-channel radio and TV, and the epidemic of smartphone distraction to shorten the patience of audiences. The laconic Lincoln would have found no problem with this, even if his lanky simian looks and clumsy, jerky movements would not have worked on screen. Yet the merging of news and entertainment has worked for some. The elegant Obama gave speeches – beautiful, almost Classical phrases, exquisite delivery (touches of Dr King), inspirational themes (echoes of Lincoln) – that carried him to the presidency. Yet his polar opposite, the bombastic Trump, is an unconventional but very successful communicator and orator, improvising long meandering speeches that delighted rallies of his supporters. They were often broadcast in full, and proved compelling even to his critics. One does not recall the phrases but the impression is authentic and unforgettable.

Trump's speechmaking highlights something bigger: today, oratory is flourishing in a way that is more visceral and popular than it ever was, even in Cicero's Rome or Pericles's Athens. Young speakers like Greta Thunberg and Malala can become instantly world-famous in one televised speech fighting for climate change reform or education. A brilliant novelist like Chimamanda Ngozi Adichie can talk about feminism as a podcast and reach millions. Speeches – or often visionbites or extracts of speeches – are viewed many millions of times on the internet. The speech has never been more powerful because television and internet have never been more dominant, while the 'old'-style media – newspapers, mainly, and trustworthy news TV – has withered dangerously. So far it is autocrats and populists who have exploited this best by appealing over the heads of traditional media directly to 'the people'. But if they can do so, others can too.

The real theme of this book is a celebration of – and warning against – the power of words. Leaders are responsible for their words, and words have consequences. The violence of language normalises the acceptability of violence, which leads inexorably towards the practice of violence. When murderous leaders like Robespierre, Lenin and Hitler spoke, they were surprisingly frank in their intentions but instead of judging them by their words, listeners ignored or downplayed their statements due to wishful thinking or fatal underestimation. Words and ideas of violence helped make the twentieth century into the century of blood.

In our age of populism, racism, antisemitism and conspiracism, we must always judge politicians by their words. 'When bad men combine,' writes Burke, 'the good must associate;

else they fall by one by one.' When Burke says 'associate', we might say, write your own speech; use your own words; find a speaker who can articulate ideas to a new audience. The fashion today is to exaggerate the evil of opponents; to accuse them of ill-defined betrayals, to dehumanise imagined 'enemies' and supposed 'outsiders' using an unsettling combination of preposterous nostalgia, invented facts, incontinent hyperbole and threats of violence. This leads to depletion of trust and respect, to further polarisation, which then makes decisions, based on compromise, ever harder. The failure to compromise can lead to the collapse of civil societies. This vicious circle is not confined to Left or Right, each echoes and mirrors the other, as if 'through a glass darkly'. Yet many of the exquisite speeches in this book prove that words can be the balm that heals wounds, the elixir for cruel times. Or the poison.

I hope in this selection you enjoy some of the finest words ever spoken – and some of the most ignoble. Words matter. Respect them – and those who use them well. Take your choice. Language is everything.

Thank you – and good night.

Simon Sebag Montefiore
London, 2020

Acknowledgements

I wish to thank those who have helped select these speeches: Jonathan Foreman, Kate Jarvis, my mother April Sebag-Montefiore, who died in November 2019 aged ninety-two, my sister-in-law Sarah Palmer-Tomkinson, F. M. Eloischari, Dr N. Zaki; my publishers Holly Harley, David Shelley, Katie Espiner, Jenny Lord, Maddy Price; agents Georgina Capel, Rachel Conway, Irene Baldoni and Simon Shaps. Thanks to my family: Santa, Lily, and Sasha, who helped with this book and to whom this is dedicated.

Author's Note

Many of these speeches are extremely long. At the cost of out-raging purists, I have edited the longest ones so that general readers may enjoy them.

Resistance

Boudicca, 'This is a woman's resolve', AD 61

A woman's rebellion. Boudicca was the queen of the Iceni tribe of British Celts. Her husband Prasutagus was king of what is now East Anglia which, along with southern Britain, had been ruled by Rome since its conquest under Emperor Claudius in AD 44. When Prasutagus died, he left the kingdom jointly to his daughters and the Roman emperor, now Nero, as was traditional for client kings. But under Nero and his corrupt henchmen, the kingdom was annexed, and the governor of Britain, Gaius Suetonius Paulinus, ordered that the widow Boudicca be flogged and her daughters raped. At the same time, the courtier and philosopher Seneca is said to have called in his British loans, adding a financial motive to the rebellion. While the governor was campaigning on the island of Anglesey off Wales, Boudicca attacked the Romans, storming the towns of Camulodunum (modern Colchester), and Londinium (London). It looked as if much of the island was lost and Nero discussed whether to abandon Britain, but his governor defeated Boudicca, who probably committed suicide. At the height of her victories, after the defeat of IX Legion, Boudicca gives this speech, recorded by the historian Tacitus, whose father-in-law Agricola was on Paulinus's staff during the revolt, so it is likely it is based on the accounts of Iceni prisoners.

It is not as a woman descended from noble ancestry, but as one of the people that I am avenging lost freedom, my scourged body, the outraged chastity of my daughters. Roman lust has gone so far that not our very persons, nor even age or virginity, are left unpolluted. But heaven is on the side of a righteous vengeance; a legion which dared to fight has perished; the rest are hiding themselves in their camp, or are thinking anxiously of flight. They will not sustain even the din and the shout of so many thousands, much less our charge and our blows.

If you weigh well the strength of the armies, and the causes of the war, you will see that in this battle you must conquer or die. This is a woman's resolve; as for men, they may live and be slaves.

Elizabeth I, 'The heart and stomach of a king', 8 August 1588

One of the great speeches of resistance – but it also faces up to the challenge of being a female leader in a very male age. After the Catholic rule of her elder half-sister Queen Mary, who had married the greatest Catholic monarch, Philip II of Spain, the throne passed to the remarkable Elizabeth, daughter of Henry VIII and Anne Boleyn. Philip, who had until recently been King of England by marriage, hoped that the young queen would at least indulge Catholics, and considered whether to marry her too. When Philip learned that Elizabeth was a devout Protestant, hostile to Spain and Catholicism and furthermore a strong politician, he planned her assassination. Elizabeth licensed her semi-official privateers, the so-called Sea Dogs (among whom was Sir Francis Drake), to raid Spanish treasure fleets, while in 1584, Spanish atrocities in Holland finally pushed her to send a small army under her favourite, the Earl of Leicester, to fight with the Dutch rebels.

Philip decided to send an armada to invade England. In 1688, 130 ships bearing 18,000 soldiers set sail to link up with a further 30,000 men in the Spanish Netherlands. Elizabeth faced panic on all sides as she mustered an army – more of a makeshift militia – at Tilbury and deployed the fleet in the Channel under admirals Lord Howard of Effingham and Drake. On 28/29 July her admirals sent in fireships that destroyed many Spanish ships and forced others out to sea. Little of the Armada returned to Spain. But before the news reaches Elizabeth, she inspects the army, accompanied by her dashing new favourite the Earl of Essex, and gives this speech. Her command of English, as seen in her many letters and speeches, is masterful. She survived the crisis, and while most histories claim Spain did not threaten England again, Philip sent two further armadas. Both failed.

My loving people,

We have been persuaded by some that are careful of our safety, to take heed how we commit ourselves to armed multitudes, for fear of treachery; but I assure you I do not desire to live to distrust my faithful and loving people. Let tyrants fear, I have always so behaved myself that, under God, I have placed my chiefest strength and safeguard in the loyal hearts and good-will of my subjects; and therefore I am come amongst you, as you see, at this time, not for my recreation and disport, but being resolved, in the midst and heat of the battle, to live and die amongst you all; to lay down for my God, and for my kingdom, and my people, my honour and my blood, even in the dust.

I know I have the body but of a weak and feeble woman; but I have the heart and stomach of a king, and of a king of England too, and think foul scorn that Parma or Spain, or any prince of Europe, should dare to invade the borders of my realm; to which rather than any dishonour shall grow by me, I myself will take up arms, I myself will be your general, judge, and rewarder of every one of your virtues in the field. I know already, for your forwardness you have deserved rewards and crowns; and We do assure you in the word of a prince, they shall be duly paid you. In the meantime, my lieutenant general shall be in my stead, than whom never prince commanded a more noble or worthy subject; not doubting but by your obedience to my general, by your concord in the camp, and your valour in the field, we shall shortly have a famous victory over those enemies of my God, of my kingdom, and of my people.

John Boyega, 'Black lives have always mattered', 3 June 2020

In May 2020 the murder by American police of an innocent Black man, George Floyd, sparked international outrage. People gathered to protest police brutality and wider racism against Black people, and the killings of Breonna Taylor (Kentucky, 2020), Sandra Bland (Texas, 2015), Trayvon Martin (Florida, 2012), Mark Duggan (London, 2011), Stephen Lawrence (London, 1993), and many others. In this speech given spontaneously at a rally, the *Star Wars* actor named some of the victims. For the first time the Black Lives Matter movement has united Black and white protestors against continuing racism in free societies. Here it is Boyega's righteous eloquence, fury, passion and humanity that makes this so powerful and poignant.

First, I want to thank every single one of you for coming out. This is very important.

This is very vital. Black lives have always mattered, we have always been important, we have always met suffering, we have always succeeded, regardless.

And now is the time. I ain't waiting. I ain't waiting.

I have been born in this country. I'm twenty-eight years old. Born and raised in London.

And for time, every Black person understands and realises the first time you were reminded that you were Black.

You remember. Every Black person in here remembered when another person reminded you that you were Black.

So none of you out there, all those protesters on the other side, protesting against what we want to do, protesting against what we want to try and achieve.

Darn you, because this is so vital. I need you guys to understand. I need you guys to understand. I need you to understand how— how painful this s**t is.

I need you to understand how painful it is. To be reminded every day that your race means nothing.

And that isn't the case anymore. There is never a case anymore. We are going to try today.

We are a physical representation of our support for George Floyd. We are a physical representation of our support for Sandra Bland.

We are a physical representation of our support for Trayvon Martin. We are a physical representation of our support for Stephen Lawrence, for Mark Duggan.

It is very, very important that we keep control of this moment and we make this as peaceful as possible.

We make this as peaceful and as organised as possible. Because you know what, guys, they want us to mess up.

They want us to be disorganised, but not today. Not today. Not today. You know what, this message is specifically for Black men. Black men.

Black men, Black men, we need to take care of our Black women. We need to take care of them.

They are ours. They are our hearts. They are our future. We cannot demonise our own.

We are the pillars of the family. Imagine this, a nation that is set up with individual families that are thriving, that are healthy, that communicate, that raise their children in love.

Have a better rate of becoming better human beings. And that's what we need to create. Black men, it starts with you.

Ay, it's done, man. We can't be trust no more. We have to be better. You lot understand? I'm speaking to you from my heart. Look, I don't know if I'm going to have a career after this, but f**k that.

This, today, is about innocent people who were halfway through their process. We don't know what George Floyd could have achieved.

We don't know what Sandra Bland could have achieved, but today we're going to make sure that that won't be an alien thought to our young ones.

I'm sure you all came today, you left your kids, and when you see your kids there, aimlessly playing, they don't understand what's going on. Today's the day that we remind them that we are dedicated, and this is a lifelong dedication.

Guys, we don't leave here and stop. We don't leave here and stop. This is longevity. Some of you are artists. Some of you are bankers. Some of you are lawyers. Some of you own shop stores. You are important.

Your individual power, your individual right is very, very important. We can all join together to make this a better world.

We can all join together to make this special. We can all join together.

Eleazar Ben Yair, 'Let us die before we become slaves', AD 73

Extreme heroism in the most desperate of times. When an entire Jewish community faced certain execution, rape and servitude, along with the crushing of their religious beliefs, their leader proposes that they should commit suicide.

It had started with the Jewish revolt against the Roman Empire: in AD 66 the brutal corruption under Emperor Nero led to a rebellion by the Jews in Jerusalem and much of present-day Israel. Jewish rebel armies defeated successive Roman legions. Faced with a rebellion in Rome itself, Nero committed suicide but before his death, he despatched an experienced general, Vespasian, to reconquer the territories.

Vespasian marched southwards methodically, taking advantage of the fact that the Jewish rebels were divided into militias who fought incessantly among themselves. While in Galilee he captured a moderate Jewish general, Josephus, who on the verge of execution predicted that Vespasian would become emperor. When he did just that, Josephus, who revered Judaism but was horrified by the excesses of the Jewish rebels, joined Vespasian's entourage. When Vespasian left to rule the empire, his son Titus besieged Jerusalem. He stormed it in AD 70, destroying the city and the Temple, killing virtually everyone, as many as 500,000 people. A small group of rebels escaped to the fortress of Masada to the south, which had originally been built as the stronghold of King Herod the Great. There a group of nearly 1,000 Jews held out until around AD 73 when the Roman governor of Judaea, Lucius Flavius Silva, laid siege to it. Masada was almost impregnable but over many months, Flavius built a vast ramp, almost a new mountain, alongside Masada to make it possible to storm the fortress.

At this point, the Jewish leader Eleazar gives this speech to persuade his people to commit suicide. Time is running out. When he finally persuades them, the men kill their wives and children, then themselves. When the Romans enter, they find 960 dead. But two women and five children had remained alive by hiding. Josephus used his access not just to the Roman generals but also the surviving Jews to write his history. It is likely that this speech is based on his conversations with the women and children who survived the suicide. It is one of the greatest speeches of all time. Masada has kept its power: today, all Israeli soldiers finish their training with a ceremony on the mountain fortress.

Since we, long ago, my generous friends, resolved never to be slaves to the Romans, nor to any other than to God himself, who alone is the true and just Lord of mankind, the time is now come that obliges us to make that resolution true in practice . . .

We were the very first that revolted against them, and we are the last that fight against them; and I cannot but regard it as a favour that God hath granted us, that it is still in our power to die bravely, and in a state of freedom, which hath not been the case of others, who were conquered unexpectedly.

It is very plain that we shall be captured within a day's time; but it is still possible to die in a glorious manner, together with our dearest friends. This is what our enemies themselves cannot by any means hinder, although they would dearly love to take us alive.

Nor can we propose to ourselves any more to fight them, and beat them. Consider how God has convinced us that our hopes were in vain, by bringing such distress upon us in the desperate state we are now in, and which is beyond all our expectations; for the nature of this fortress which was in itself unconquerable, has not proved a means of our deliverance; and even while we have still great abundance of food, and a great quantity of arms, and other necessaries more than we want, we are openly deprived by God himself of all hope of deliverance . . .

But first let us destroy our money and the fortress by fire; for I am well assured that this will be a great grief to the Romans, that they shall not be able to seize upon our bodies, and shall miss our wealth also; and let us spare nothing but our provisions; for they will be a testimonial when we are dead that we were not subdued for want of provisions, but that, according to our own choice, we have preferred death before slavery.

Here those assembled resisted his argument.

Truly, I was greatly mistaken when I thought I was helping brave men, who fought hard for their freedom, and were therefore resolved to live with honour or else die. But I find that you are such people no better than any others, either in virtue or in courage, and are afraid of dying, though you would be saved that way from the greatest miseries, while you ought to make no delay in this matter, nor to await any one to give you good advice. For the laws of our country, and of God himself, have from ancient times, and as soon as ever we could use our reason, continually taught us . . . that it is life that is a calamity to men, and not death; for this last affords our souls their liberty, and sends them by a removal into their own place of purity, where they are to be insensible of all sorts of misery. For while souls are tied down to a mortal body, they share its miseries; and really, to speak the truth, they are themselves dead; for the union of what is divine to what is mortal is disagreeable . . .

The circumstances we are now in ought to be an inducement to us to bear such calamity courageously, since it is by the will of God, and by necessity, that we are to die; for it now appears that God hath made such a ruling against the whole Jewish nation, that we are to be deprived of this life. Look at those that are now under the Romans: who would not pity their condition? And who would not make haste to die, before he would suffer the same miseries with them? Some of them have been put upon the rack, and tortured with fire and whippings, and so died. Some have been half devoured by wild beasts, and yet have been kept alive to be devoured by them a second time, in order to afford laughter and sport to our enemies; and such of those as are alive still are to be looked on as the most miserable, who, being so desirous of death, could not come at it. And where is now that great city [Jerusalem], the metropolis of the Jewish nation, which was fortified by so many walls round about, which had so many fortresses and large towers to defend it, which could hardly contain the instruments prepared for the war, and which had so many ten thousands of men to fight for it? Where is this city in which it was believed God himself resided? It is now demolished to the very foundations, and hath nothing but that monument of it preserved, I mean the camp of those who destroyed it, who still dwell upon its ruins; some unfortunate old men also lie upon the ashes of the Temple, and a few women are there preserved alive by the enemy, for our bitter shame and reproach. Now who is there that revolves these things in his mind, and yet is able to bear the sight of the sun, though he might live out of danger? Who is there so much his country's enemy, or so unmanly, and so desirous of living, as not to repent that he is still alive? And I cannot but wish that we had all died before we had seen that Holy City demolished by the hands of our enemies, or the foundations of our holy Temple dug up in such a profane manner.

Let us pity ourselves, our children, and our wives while it is in our own power to show pity to them; for we were born to die, as well as those were whom we have begotten; nor is it in the power of the most happy of our race to avoid it. But for abuses, and slavery, and the sight of our wives led away in an ignominious manner, with their children, these are not such evils as are natural and necessary among men; although such as do not prefer death before those miseries, when it is in their power so to do, must undergo even them, on account of their own cowardice.

We revolted from the Romans with great pretensions to courage; and when, at the very last, they invited us to preserve ourselves, we would not comply with them. Who will not, therefore, believe that they will certainly be in a rage at us, in case they can take us alive? . . . Our hands are still at liberty, and have a sword in them; let them then be subservient to us in our glorious design; let us die before we become slaves under our enemies, and let us go out of the world, together with our children and our wives, in a state of freedom ... Let us hurry, and instead of affording them so much pleasure, as they hope for in getting us under their power, let us leave them an example which shall at once cause their astonishment at our death, and their admiration for our courage.

Winston Churchill, 'Blood, toil, tears and sweat', 13 May 1940

The cause is noble – nothing less than the survival of decency, democracy and civilisation – in an era of barbarism and killing. The theme is that the war is dire, the struggle desperate and will become more so – but somehow victory will come in the end under the leadership of the speaker. Over a long career in government, starting in 1906 and including service in most high offices, Churchill had gained a mixed reputation for impulsive creativity, brazen ambition, intellectual brilliance, military adventurism, imperial sentimentality, quixotic indulgence, strategic vision, felicitous writing and fine oratory. Throughout the thirties, he almost alone, his career apparently over, had warned about the real nature of Hitler and the threat of Nazism. As soon as Prime Minister Neville Chamberlain found himself in a war he thought he had prevented, he was forced to bring Churchill into government as First Lord of the Admiralty.

As Hitler defeated France, knocking out Britain's main ally, Chamberlain was totally discredited. Churchill succeeded Chamberlain on 10 May 1940. All his life he had prepared for this moment. As a younger man, his lisp and slight stammer had made him work on his speechmaking. In the Commons, his oratory sometimes seemed antique and long-winded. But he wrote and rewrote his speeches with immense care, his mastery of English was unparalleled and he learned how to use his voice as a theatrical device. 'It was the nation and the race dwelling all round the globe that had the lion's heart,' he wrote later. 'I had the luck to be called upon to give the roar.' As Prime Minister he believed 'all my past life had been but a preparation for this hour.' On 13 May, he addresses the House of Commons. His speech is a masterpiece.

On Friday evening last I received His Majesty's commission to form a new administration. It was the evident wish and will of Parliament and the nation that this should be conceived on the broadest possible basis and that it should include all parties . . . I have completed the most important part of this task.

. . . I now invite the House, by the resolution that stands in my name, to record its approval of the steps taken and declare its confidence in the new government. The resolution is: 'That this House welcomes the formation of a government representing the united and inflexible resolve of the nation to prosecute the war with Germany to a victorious conclusion.'

To form an administration of this scale and complexity is a serious undertaking in itself, but it must be remembered that we are in the preliminary stage of one of the greatest battles in history, that we are in action at many points in Norway and in Holland, that we have to be prepared in the Mediterranean, that the air battle is continuous and that many preparations have to be made here at home.

In this crisis I hope I may be pardoned if I do not address the House at any length today, and I hope that any of my friends and colleagues or former colleagues who are affected by the political reconstruction will make all allowances for any lack of ceremony with which it has been necessary to act.

I would say to the House, as I said to ministers who have joined this government, 'I have nothing to offer but blood, toil, tears and sweat.' We have before us an ordeal of the most grievous kind. We have before us many, many long months of struggle and of suffering.

You ask, what is our policy? I can say: it is to wage war by sea, land and air, with all our might and with all the strength God can give us; to wage war against a monstrous tyranny, never surpassed in the dark and lamentable catalogue of human crime. That is our policy.

You ask, what is our aim? I can answer in one word. It is victory; victory at all costs, victory in spite of all terror, victory, however long and hard the road may be; for without victory, there is no survival.

Let that be realized; no survival for the British Empire, no survival for all that the British Empire has stood for, no survival for the urge and impulse of the ages, that mankind will move forward towards its goal.

But I take up my task with buoyancy and hope. I feel sure that our cause will not be suffered to fail among men. At this time I feel entitled to claim the aid of all, and I say, 'Come then, let us go forward together with our united strength.'

Emmeline Pankhurst, 'I am here as a soldier', 13 November 1913

'Freedom or death' was the choice posed by Pankhurst, the leader of the Suffragist movement that campaigned for women's right to vote at the turn of the twentieth century. Emmeline Pankhurst (née Goulden) was married to Richard Pankhurst, who also campaigned for female rights. Richard died in 1889 but Pankhurst continued to play the lead role in a celebrated campaign of what she called 'deeds not words'. In 1903, Emmeline founded the Women's Social and Political Union with her daughters Christabel, Adele and Sylvia. From throwing axes at the prime minister to breaking the windows in Downing Street and fighting with police, the struggle intensified. When she was in prison, Pankhurst led hunger strikes to which the authorities reacted by the horrendous trauma of forced feeding to keep the Suffragists alive. Introducing herself as a 'hooligan', Pankhurst made her first visit to the US in 1909 and now, in 1913, released from jail, she returns to America to give this speech. The First World War achieved what Pankhurst's measures had not. Pankhurst called a halt to the protests to back the war. The Suffragists were released, and the service of women during the war changed the way women's rights were viewed. In June 1918, an Act of Parliament gave women over the age of thirty the right to vote (with restrictions). A Parliamentary bill giving women equal voting rights to men became law in July 1928 – the month after Emmeline died.

I do not come here as an advocate, because whatever position the suffrage movement may occupy in the United States of America, in England it has passed beyond the realm of advocacy and it has entered into the sphere of practical politics. It has become the subject of revolution and civil war, and so tonight I am not here to advocate woman suffrage.

American suffragists can do that very well for themselves. I am here as a soldier who has temporarily left the field of battle in order to explain – it seems strange it should have to be explained – what civil war is like when civil war is waged by women . . . If I were a man and I said to you, 'I come from a country which professes to have representative institutions and yet denies me, a taxpayer, an inhabitant of the country, representative rights,' you would at once understand that that human being, being a man, was justified in the adoption of revolutionary methods to get representative institutions. But since I am a woman it is necessary in the twentieth century to explain why women have adopted revolutionary methods in order to win the rights of citizenship.

. . . Now, I want to say to you who think women cannot succeed, we have brought the government of England to this position, that it has to face this alternative: either women are to be killed or women are to have the vote. I ask American men in this meeting, what would you say if in your State you were faced with that alternative, that you must either kill them or give them their citizenship – women, many of whom you respect, women whom you know have lived useful lives, women whom you know, even if you do not know them personally, are animated with the highest motives, women who are in pursuit of liberty and the power to do useful public service? Well, there is only one answer to that alternative; there is only one way out of it, unless you are prepared to put back civilization two or three generations: you must give those women the vote. Now that is the outcome of our civil war.

Dreamers

Martin Luther King, Jr, 'I have a dream', 28 August 1963

The speech that expresses African-American civil rights – and a freer, more equal, more inclusive version of the white American Dream. Even in the twenty-first century, the speech feels fresh and relevant. The words are beautiful and inspiring but the original speech was entitled 'Normalcy, Never Again' and did not contain the 'I have a dream' climax. Highly influenced by speakers such as Lincoln and the tradition of black evangelical preaching, King was the son of a preacher from Atlanta, Georgia. He acquired a PhD in theology and became a Baptist preacher himself before emerging as one of the leaders of the civil rights movement in the South, where a century after Civil War and black emancipation, African-Americans were still widely segregated and oppressed by the Jim Crow Laws.

In 1955, King led the Montgomery bus boycott, during which Rosa Parks challenged the law of segregation on Alabama buses, then as first president of the Southern Christian Leadership Conference, King confronted segregation in Georgia and organised protests in Birmingham, Alabama.

In August 1963, King is one of the leaders of the March on Washington, at which he speaks to 250,000 marchers outside the Lincoln Memorial. The marchers call for an end to segregation and discrimination. This speech is so strong because, unlike most orations, it contains several peaks – just when you think it cannot get better, it does. Filled with deliberate archaisms and evangelical cadences, Biblical references and spiritual echoes, it is rich in treasures. It is pervaded with the shame that the American New Jerusalem has so failed its people. He had played with the idea of his dream in many speeches, so he knows the words when the American gospel singer Mahalia Jackson calls out: 'Tell them about the dream, Martin!' King starts to improvise. It is a tour de force, perhaps the greatest speech in this collection. Yet his time was limited.

Five score years ago, a great American, in whose symbolic shadow we stand today, signed the Emancipation Proclamation. This momentous decree came as a great beacon light of hope to millions of negro slaves, who had been seared in the flames of withering injustice. It came as a joyous daybreak to end the long night of their captivity.

But one hundred years later, the negro still is not free. One hundred years later, the life of the negro is still sadly crippled by the manacles of segregation and the chains of discrimination. One hundred years later, the negro lives on a lonely island of poverty in the midst of a vast ocean of material prosperity. One hundred years later, the negro still languishes in the corners of American society and finds himself an exile in his own land. And so we've come here today to dramatize a shameful condition . . .

But we refuse to believe that the bank of justice is bankrupt. We refuse to believe that there are insufficient funds in the great vaults of opportunity of this nation. And so we have come to cash this cheque, a cheque that will give us upon demand the riches of freedom and the security of justice.

We have also come to this hallowed spot to remind America of the fierce urgency of Now. This is no time to engage in the luxury of cooling off or to take the tranquillizing drug of gradualism. Now is the time to make real the promises of democracy. Now is the time to rise from the dark and desolate valley of segregation to the sunlit path of racial justice. Now is the time to lift our nation from the quicksands of racial injustice to the solid rock of brotherhood. Now is the time to make justice a reality for all of God's children.

It would be fatal for the nation to overlook the urgency of the moment. This sweltering summer of the negro's legitimate discontent will not pass until there is an invigorating autumn of freedom and equality. Nineteen sixty-three is not an end but a beginning. Those who hope that the negro needed to blow off steam and will now be content will have a rude awakening if the nation returns to business as usual. There will be neither rest nor tranquillity in America until the negro is granted his citizenship rights. The whirlwinds of revolt will continue to shake the foundations of our nation until the bright day of justice emerges.

But there is something that I must say to my people who stand on the warm threshold which leads into the palace of justice. In the process of gaining our rightful place we must not be guilty of wrongful deeds. Let us not seek to satisfy our thirst for freedom by drinking from the cup of bitterness and hatred. We must ever conduct our struggle on the high plane of dignity and discipline. We must not allow our creative protest to degenerate into physical violence. Again and again we must rise to the majestic heights of meeting physical force with soul force.

The marvellous new militancy which has engulfed the negro community must not lead us to a distrust of all white people, for many of our white brothers, as evidenced by their presence here today, have come to realize that their destiny is tied up with our destiny. And they have come to realize that their freedom is inextricably bound to our freedom. We cannot walk alone.

And as we walk, we must make the pledge that we shall always march ahead. We cannot turn back. There are those who are asking the devotees of civil rights, 'When will you be satisfied?' We can never be satisfied as long as the negro is the victim of the unspeakable horrors of police brutality. We can never be satisfied as long as our bodies, heavy with the fatigue of travel, cannot gain lodging in the motels of the highways and the hotels of the cities. We cannot be satisfied as long as a negro in Mississippi cannot vote and a negro in New York believes he has nothing for which to vote. No, no, we are not satisfied and we will not be satisfied until justice rolls down like waters and righteous-ness like a mighty stream.

I am not unmindful that some of you have come here out of great trials and tribulations. Some of you have come fresh from narrow jail cells.

Some of you have come from areas where your quest for freedom left you battered by the storms of persecutions and staggered by the winds of police brutality. You have been the veterans of creative suffering.

Continue to work with the faith that unearned suffering is redemptive. Go back to Mississippi, go back to Alabama, go back to South Carolina, go back to Georgia, go back to Louisiana, go back to the slums and ghettos of our northern cities, knowing that somehow this situation can and will be changed. Let us not wallow in the valley of despair, I say to you today, my friends. And so even though we face the difficulties of today and tomorrow, I still have a dream. It is a dream deeply rooted in the American dream.

I have a dream that one day this nation will rise up and live out the true meaning of its creed: We hold these truths to be self-evident that all men are created equal.

I have a dream that one day on the red hills of Georgia the sons of former slaves and the sons of former slave owners will be able to sit down together at the table of brotherhood.

I have a dream that one day even the state of Mississippi, a state sweltering with the heat of injustice, sweltering with the heat of oppression, will be transformed into an oasis of freedom and justice.

I have a dream that my four little children will one day live in a nation where they will not be judged by the colour of their skin but by the content of their character. I have a dream today!

I have a dream that one day, down in Alabama, with its vicious racists, with its governor having his lips dripping with the words of interposition and nullification; one day right down in Alabama little black boys and black girls will be able to join hands with little white boys and white girls as sisters and brothers. I have a dream today!

I have a dream that one day every valley shall be exalted, and every hill and mountain shall be made low, the rough places will be made plain, and the crooked places will be made straight, and the glory of the Lord shall be revealed and all flesh shall see it together.

This is our hope. This is the faith that I will go back to the South with. With this faith we will be able to hew out of the mountain of despair a stone of hope. With this faith we will be able to transform the jangling discords of our nation into a beautiful symphony of brotherhood. With this faith we will be able to work together, to pray together, to struggle together, to go to jail together, to stand up for freedom together, knowing that we will be free one day. And this will be the day, this will be the day when all of God's children will be able to sing with new meaning, 'My country 'tis of thee, sweet land of liberty, of thee I sing. Land where my fathers died, land of the Pilgrim's pride, from every mountainside, let freedom ring!' And if America is to be a great nation, this must become true.

And so let freedom ring from the prodigious hilltops of New Hampshire. Let freedom ring from the mighty mountains of New York.

Let freedom ring from the heightening Alleghenies of Pennsylvania. Let freedom ring from the snow-capped Rockies of Colorado.

Let freedom ring from the curvaceous slopes of California.

But not only that. Let freedom ring from Stone Mountain of Georgia. Let freedom ring from Lookout Mountain of Tennessee.

Let freedom ring from every hill and molehill of Mississippi, from every mountainside, let freedom ring!

And when this happens, when we allow freedom to ring, when we let it ring from every village and every hamlet, from every state and every city, we will be able to speed up that day when all of God's children, black men and white men, Jews and Gentiles, Protestants and Catholics, will be able to join hands and sing in the words of the old negro spiritual, 'Free at last, free at last. Thank God Almighty, we are free at last.'

Sojourner Truth, 'Ain't I a woman?'
1863 version recorded by Frances Dana Barker Gage

One speech, two very different versions. Sojourner Truth was not her real name. She was born Isabella Baumfree, an African-American slave in Ulster County, New York, where she spoke Dutch as well as English. Sold four times to different masters, once at an auction for $100 with some sheep, she suffered all the cruelties of slavery. She had children with a fellow slave and managed to escape slavery in 1826 with one of them, when the institution was on the verge of abolition in New York. But she had to leave her sons to serve as bound servants. Later she learned one of her sons had been illegally sold to slavery in Alabama and successfully went to court and got him back, the first black woman to win a court case against a white man. Her son later joined a whaling ship and vanished. At one point she joined a so-called Prophet Matthias in a religious cult but in 1843, she embraced Methodism and took the name Sojourner Truth, campaigning for the abolition of slavery and for women's rights, inspired by God.

In 1851, she gives this speech at the Women's Rights Convention in Akron, Ohio, which became known by her question: 'Ain't I a woman?' She speaks spontaneously and two versions of her speech exist. The first was recorded by Reverend Marius Robinson who was present and is couched in conventional English, but later – in 1863 during the Civil War – Frances Gage, who was also present, published the more famous version that includes the phrase 'Ain't I a woman?' Introduced by Gage, the speech is expressed in a Southern black dialect that a white audience might expect from a former slave.

The leaders of the movement trembled on seeing a tall, gaunt black woman in a gray dress and white turban, surmounted with an uncouth sunbonnet, march deliberately into the church, walk with the air of a queen up the aisle, and take her seat upon the pulpit steps. A buzz of disapprobation was heard all over the house, and there fell on the listening ear, 'An abolition affair!', 'Woman's rights and niggers!', 'I told you so!', 'Go it, darkey!'. Again and again, timorous and trembling ones came to me and said, with earnestness, 'Don't let her speak, Mrs. Gage, it will ruin us. Every newspaper in the land will have our cause mixed up with abolition and niggers, and we shall be utterly denounced.' My only answer was, 'We shall see when the time comes.'

The second day the work waxed warm. Methodist, Baptist, Episcopal, Presbyterian, and Universalist ministers came in to hear and discuss the resolutions presented. One claimed superior rights and privileges for man, on the ground of 'superior intellect'; another, because of the 'manhood of Christ; if God had desired the equality of woman, He would have given some token of His will through the birth, life, and death of the Saviour.' Another gave us a theological view of the 'sin of our first mother.'

There were very few women in those days who dared to 'speak in meeting'; and the august teachers of the people were seemingly getting the better of us, while the boys in the galleries, and the sneerers among the pews, were hugely enjoying the discomfiture as they supposed, of the 'strong-minded.' Some of the tender-skinned friends were on the point of losing dignity, and the atmosphere betokened a storm. When, slowly from her seat in the corner rose Sojourner Truth, who, till now, had scarcely lifted her head. 'Don't let her speak!' gasped half a dozen in my ear. She moved slowly and solemnly to the front, laid her old bonnet at her feet, and turned her great speaking eyes to me. There was a hissing sound of disapprobation above and below. I rose and announced, 'Sojourner Truth,' and begged the audience to keep silence for a few moments.

The tumult subsided at once, and every eye was fixed on this almost Amazon form, which stood nearly six feet high, head erect, and eyes piercing the upper air like one in a dream. At her first word there was a profound hush. She spoke in deep tones, which, though not loud, reached every ear in the house, and away through the throng at the doors and windows.

'Wall, chilern, whar dar is so much racket dar must be somethin' out o' kilter. I tink dat 'twixt de niggers of de Souf and de womin at de Norf, all talkin' 'bout rights, de white men will be in a fix pretty soon. But what's all dis here talkin' 'bout?

'Dat man ober dar say dat womin needs to be helped into carriages, and lifted ober ditches, and to hab de best place everywhar. Nobody eber helps me into carriages, or ober mud-puddles, or gibs me any best place!' And raising herself to her full height, and her voice to a pitch like rolling thunder, she asked, 'And ain't I a woman? Look at me! Look at my arm! [and she bared her right arm to the shoulder, showing her tremendous muscular power]. I have ploughed, and planted, and gathered into barns, and no man could head me! And ain't I a woman? I could work as much and eat as much as a man – when I could get it – and bear de lash as well! And ain't I a woman? I have borne thirteen chilern, and seen 'em mos' all sold off to slavery, and when I cried out with my mother's grief, none but Jesus heard me! And ain't I a woman?

'Den dey talks 'bout dis ting in de head; what dis dey call it? ['Intellect,' whispered someone near.] Dat's it, honey. What's dat got to do wid womin's rights or nigger's rights? If my cup won't hold but a pint, and yourn holds a quart, wouldn't ye be mean not to let me have my little half-measure full?' And she pointed her significant finger, and sent a keen glance at the minister who had made the argument. The cheering was long and loud.

'Den dat little man in black dar, he say women can't have as much rights as men, 'cause Christ wan't a woman! Whar did your Christ come from?' Rolling thunder couldn't have stilled that crowd, as did those deep, wonderful tones, as she stood there with outstretched arms and eyes of fire. Raising her voice still louder, she repeated, 'Whar did your Christ come from? From God and a woman! Man had nothin' to do wid Him.' Oh, what a rebuke that was to that little man.

Turning again to another objector, she took up the defense of Mother Eve. I cannot follow her through it all. It was pointed, and witty, and solemn; eliciting at almost every sentence deafening applause; and she ended by asserting: 'If de fust woman God ever made was strong enough to turn de world upside down all alone, dese women togedder [she glanced her eye over the platform] ought to be able to turn it back, and get it right side up again! And now dey is asking to do it, de men better let 'em.' Long-continued cheering greeted this. 'Bleeged to ye for hearin' on me, and now ole Sojourner han't got nothin' more to say.'

Muhammad Ali, 'Wait till you see Muhammad Ali', 30 October 1974

The sportsman who had a gift for oratory, Muhammad Ali, born Cassius Clay in Louisville, Kentucky in 1942, enjoyed delivering speeches and poems that he wrote before his big fights. He always called himself 'The Greatest' but he was right – he was much more than just a sportsman. He won his first world heavyweight championship from Sonny Liston at the age of twenty-two in 1964. Soon afterwards he converted to Islam, disdaining his 'slave name' Cassius Clay to become Muhammad Ali and a hero for African-Americans and a pillar of the civil rights movement. He refused to fight in the Vietnam War, for which he was temporarily stripped of his titles. He fought Liston twice, then beat rivals such as Joe Frazier and George Foreman. It was before his fight against the latter, held in Zaire (now the Democratic Republic of the Congo) and known as the Rumble in the Jungle, that he delivered his best lines: 'Float like a butterfly sting like a bee – his hands can't hit what his eyes can't see.' But this rhyming speech is his best. He finally retired from boxing aged thirty-nine, and was diagnosed with Parkinson's disease three years later in 1984. He died in 2016.

Last night I had a dream,
When I got to Africa,
I had one hell of a rumble.
I had to beat Tarzan's behind first,
For claiming to be King of the Jungle.
For this fight, I've wrestled with alligators,
I've tussled with a whale.
I done handcuffed lightning
And throw thunder in jail.
You know I'm bad.

Just last week, I murdered a rock,
Injured a stone, Hospitalized a brick.
I'm so mean, I make medicine sick.
I'm so fast, man,
I can run through a hurricane and don't get wet.
When George Foreman meets me,
He'll pay his debt.
I can drown the drink of water, and kill a dead tree.
Wait till you see Muhammad Ali.

Michelle Obama, 'Be the very best that you can be', 2 April 2009

Inspiration and aspiration for girls. Michelle Obama, the charismatic First Lady of America, visits a London inner-city state school where over 90 per cent of the pupils were from a black or minority ethnic background, on her first presidential visit to Britain. She abandons her prepared text and instead talks passionately about education and ambition. It has become a classic.

This is my first trip, my first foreign trip as a First Lady. Can you believe that? And while this is not my first visit to the UK, I have to say that I am glad that this is my first official visit . . .

And I'm honoured to meet you, the future leaders of Great Britain and this world. And although the circumstances of our lives may seem very distant, with me standing here as the First Lady of the United States of America, and you, just getting through school, I want you to know that we have very much in common. For nothing in my life's path would have predicted that I'd be standing here as the first African-American First Lady of the United States of America. There is nothing in my story that would land me here. I wasn't raised with wealth or resources or any social standing to speak of. I was raised on the South Side of Chicago. That's the real part of Chicago. And I was the product of a working-class community. My father was a city worker all of his life, and my mother was a stay-at-home mom. And she stayed at home to take care of me and my older brother. Neither of them attended university. My dad was diagnosed with multiple sclerosis in the prime of his life. But even as it got harder for him to walk and get dressed in the morning – I saw him struggle more and more – my father never complained about his struggle. He was grateful for what he had. He just woke up a little earlier and worked a little harder. And my brother and I were raised with all that you really need: love, strong values and a belief that with a good education and a whole lot of hard work, that there was nothing that we could not do.

I am an example of what's possible when girls from the very beginning of their lives are loved and nurtured by the people around them. I was surrounded by extraordinary women in my life: grandmothers, teachers, aunts, cousins, neighbours, who taught me about quiet strength and dignity. And my mother, the most important role model in my life, who lives with us at the White House and helps to care for our two little daughters, Malia and Sasha. She's an active presence in their lives, as well as mine, and is instilling in them the same values that she taught me and my brother: things like compassion, and integrity, and confidence, and perseverance – all of that wrapped up in an unconditional love that only a grandmother can give.

I was also fortunate enough to be cherished and encouraged by some strong male role models as well, including my father, my brother, uncles and grandfathers. The men in my life taught me some important things, as well. They taught me about what a respectful relationship should look like between men and women. They taught me about what a strong marriage feels like: that it's built on faith and commitment and an admiration for each other's unique gifts. They taught me about what it means to be a father and to raise a family. And not only to invest in your own home but to reach out and help raise kids in the broader community.

And these were the same qualities that I looked for in my own husband, Barack Obama . . . You are the women who will build the world as it should be. You're going to write the next chapter in history. Not just for yourselves, but for your generation and generations to come. And that's why getting a good education is so important. That's why all of this that you're going through – the ups and the downs, the teachers that you love and the teachers that you don't – why it's so important. Because communities and countries and ultimately the world are only as strong as the health of their women. And that's important to keep in mind. Part of that health includes an outstanding education . . .

And this school, named after the UK's first female doctor, and the surrounding buildings named for Mexican artist Frida Kahlo, Mary Seacole, the Jamaican nurse known as the 'black Florence Nightingale', and the English author, Emily Brontë, honour women who fought sexism, racism and ignorance, to pursue their passions to feed their own souls. They allowed for no obstacles. As the sign said back there, 'without limitations.' They knew no other way to live than to follow their dreams. And having done so, these women moved many obstacles. And they opened many new doors for millions of female doctors and nurses and artists and authors, all of whom have followed them. And by getting a good education, you too can control your own destiny.

Please remember that. If you want to know the reason why I'm standing here, it's because of education. I never cut class. Sorry, I don't know if anybody is cutting class. I never did it. I loved getting As. I liked being smart. I liked being on time. I liked getting my work done. I thought being smart was cooler than anything in the world. And you too, with these same values, can control your own destiny. You too can pave the way. You too can realize your dreams, and then your job is to reach back and to help someone just like you do the same thing. History proves that it doesn't matter whether you come from a council estate or a country estate.

Your success will be determined by your own fortitude, your own confidence, your own individual hard work. That is true. That is the reality of the world that we live in. You now have control over your own destiny. And it won't be easy – that's for sure. But you have everything you need. Everything you need to succeed, you already have, right here.

My husband works in this big office. They call it the Oval Office. In the White House, there's the desk that he sits at – it's called the Resolute desk. It was built by the timber of Her Majesty's Ship *Resolute* and given by Queen Victoria. It's an enduring symbol of the friendship between our two nations. And its name, Resolute, is a reminder of the strength of character that's required not only to lead a country, but to live a life of purpose, as well. And I hope in pursuing your dreams, you all remain resolute, that you go forward without limits, and that you use your talents – because there are many; we've seen them; it's there – that you use them to create the world as it should be. Because we are counting on you. We are counting on every single one of you to be the very best that you can be. Because the world is big. And it's full of challenges. And we need strong, smart, confident young women to stand up and take the reins.

We know you can do it, we love you. Thank you so much.

Freedom

Simón Bolívar, 'We are not Europeans; we are not Indians; we are but a mixed species', 15 February 1819

The vision of a new world by its liberator. Bolívar was born in 1783 to vast wealth in a powerful creole family in Caracas, Venezuela but devoted his life to freeing South America from Spanish rule. A child of the Enlightenment, he enjoyed adventures and love affairs in Madrid and Paris before returning home and launching his war of independence in 1808. The struggle was savage, the distances and scale of the territories were continental, thousands were killed, but he was confident in his own destiny, often saying, 'I am the genius of the storm.' He was slim and handsome, and as happy on the battlefield as he was writing or orating or making love to his many mistresses. He first liberated territories that are now Venezuela, Colombia and Panama and then expanded the war across the Andes. In an astonishing act of will and leadership he liberated Peru, Ecuador and Bolivia too. However one measures his achievements, only Napoleon Bonaparte, his contemporary, came close to those of Bolívar. When he and his revolutionary leaders meet at the Congress of Angostura to decide on the nature of a new state that they call Gran Colombia, he gives this address and is elected president.

Bolívar tried for ten years to govern Gran Colombia – effectively half of South America – but it all ended in resignation and disappointment. He died soon afterwards.

We are not Europeans; we are not Indians; we are but a mixed species of aborigines and Spaniards. Americans by birth and Europeans by law, we find ourselves engaged in a dual conflict: we are disputing with the natives for titles of ownership, and at the same time we are struggling to maintain ourselves in the country that gave us birth against the opposition of the invaders. Thus our position is most extraordinary and complicated. But there is more. As our role has always been strictly passive and political existence nil, we find that our quest for liberty is now even more difficult of accomplishment; for we, having been placed in a state lower than slavery, have been robbed not only of our freedom but also of the right to exercise an active domestic tyranny . . .

We have been ruled more by deceit than by force, and we have been degraded more by vice than by superstition. Slavery is the daughter of darkness: an ignorant people is a blind instrument of its own destruction. Ambition and intrigue abuse the credulity and experience of men lacking all political, economic, and civic knowledge; they adopt pure illusion as reality; they take licence for liberty, treachery for patriotism, and vengeance for justice. If a people, perverted by their training, succeed in achieving their liberty, they will soon lose it, for it would be of no avail to endeavour to explain to them that happiness consists in the practice of virtue; that the rule of law is more powerful than the rule of tyrants, because, as the laws are more inflexible, everyone should submit to their beneficent austerity; that proper morals, and not force, are the basis of law; and that to practise justice is to practise liberty.

Toussaint Louverture, 'I want liberty and equality to reign', 29 August 1793

The speech that heralds the first black republic of freed slaves is short, simple and exuberant. Francois-Dominique Toussaint was a slave in the French colony of Saint-Domingue on the island of Hispaniola. He was born into slavery but manumitted by his master and became the manager of a plantation, educating himself, studying Western and creole medicine, and ultimately buying his own estate which had its own slaves. Inspired by the French Enlightenment and by the drama of the French Revolution, he became the leader of a slave rebellion, earning the nickname L'Ouverture – 'the Opener' – for his military prowess.

On 29 August 1793, while still claiming loyalty to the French king Louis XVI who was by then imprisoned in Paris, Louverture reads this declaration from his Camp Turel to his fellow rebels of Saint-Domingue. But his forces were weak. He became Governor-General then autocrat for life, issuing a constitution while still formally remaining under France. The new French dictator, Napoleon Bonaparte, sent an army to crush Toussaint who in 1802 was betrayed, arrested and shipped back to France where he died in prison. Yet within a year, his creation Haiti was independent.

Brothers and friends, I am Toussaint Louverture; perhaps my name has made itself known to you. I have undertaken vengeance. I want liberty and equality to reign in Saint-Domingue. I am working to make that happen. Unite yourselves to us, brothers and fight with us for the same cause.

Your very humble and obedient servant, Toussaint Louverture. General of the armies of the king, for the public good.

Jawaharlal Nehru, 'At the stroke of the midnight hour', 14 August 1947

This speech marking the independence of India, the second largest nation in the world and the greatest democracy, is elegant, graceful and calm but the creation of the new country and the retreat of the empire that had ruled it for two centuries were bloody, messy and panic-stricken.

Britain had dominated the Indian sub-continent since the mid-eighteenth century, ruling through a viceroy since the Indian Mutiny of 1856. In the 1880s Indians founded a National Congress Party to canvass for representation and education. Pressure on Britain to concede power to Indians increased after the First World War. Congress wanted some form of independence. The struggle was led by two English-trained lawyers: Gandhi, the ascetic and spiritual champion of peaceful protest, son of a poor family, and Nehru, the exuberant and worldly moderniser with socialist sympathies, a middle-class Old Harrovian. Britain resisted but atrocities like General Dyer's shooting of almost 400 unarmed demonstrators at Amritsar in 1919 added to the momentum. Both leaders were in and out of prison frequently.

By 1945, Britain was exhausted by the Second World War and the new Labour government ordered the last viceroy, Lord Mountbatten, to negotiate immediate Indian independence. The rushed creation of two new states, India and Pakistan, Hindu and Muslim respectively, was accompanied by huge movements of population and appalling massacres in which as many as a million perished. This speech is a superb piece of rhetoric. The phrase 'tryst with destiny' is strong but the power lies in Nehru's romantic deployment of the very time of independence – midnight – the moment that India awakens.

Long years ago we made a tryst with destiny, and now the time comes when we shall redeem our pledge, not wholly or in full measure, but very substantially.

At the stroke of the midnight hour, when the world sleeps, India will awake to life and freedom. A moment comes, which comes but rarely in history, when we step out from the old to the new, when an age ends, and when the soul of a nation, long suppressed, finds utterance. It is fitting that at this solemn moment we take the pledge of dedication to the service of India and her people and to the still larger cause of humanity.

At the dawn of history India started on her unending quest, and trackless centuries are filled with her striving and the grandeur of her success and her failures. Through good and ill fortune alike she has never lost sight of that quest or forgotten the ideals which gave her strength. We end today a period of ill fortune and India discovers herself again. The achievement we celebrate today is but a step, an opening of opportunity, to the greater triumphs and achievements that await us. Are we brave enough and wise enough to grasp this opportunity and accept the challenge of the future?

. . . To the people of India, whose representatives we are, we make an appeal to join us with faith and confidence in this great adventure. This is no time for petty and destructive criticism, no time for ill will or blaming others.

We have to build the noble mansion of free India where all her children may dwell.

Nelson Mandela, 'Rainbow nation', 10 May 1994

A rare example of a man who deserves his reputation for nobility, Mandela survived thirty years' imprisonment through force of character and clarity of mission. In 1991, he was finally freed from prison as the Nationalist Party under President F. W. de Klerk moved towards the abolition of apartheid, the racist system by which the white minority had enforced its rule in South Africa since 1946. The long-awaited elections took place in May 1994. Mandela was elected to the presidency and his victory speech, inspired partly by Martin Luther King, reveals his generosity of spirit: the bloodless transition of power in South Africa was a miracle. And that was all due to Mandela.

Your majesties, your highnesses, distinguished guests, comrades and friends:

Today, all of us do, by our presence here, and by our celebrations in other parts of our country and the world, confer glory and hope to newborn liberty.

Out of the experience of an extraordinary human disaster that lasted too long, must be born a society of which all humanity will be proud.

Our daily deeds as ordinary South Africans must produce an actual South African reality that will reinforce humanity's belief in justice, strengthen its confidence in the nobility of the human soul and sustain all our hopes for glorious life for all.

All this we owe both to ourselves and to the peoples of the world who are so well represented here today.

To my compatriots, I have no hesitation in saying that each one of us is as intimately attached to the soil of this beautiful country as are the famous jacaranda trees of Pretoria and the mimosa trees of the bushveld.

Each time one of us touches the soil of this land, we feel a sense of personal renewal. The national mood changes as the seasons change.

We are moved by a sense of joy and exhilaration when the grass turns green and the flowers bloom.

That spiritual and physical oneness we all share with this common homeland explains the depth of the pain we all carried in our hearts as we saw our country tear itself apart in a terrible conflict, and as we saw it spurned, outlawed and isolated by the peoples of the world, precisely because it had become the universal base of the pernicious ideology and practice of racism and racial oppression.

We, the people of South Africa, feel fulfilled that humanity has taken us back into its bosom, that we, who were outlaws not so long ago, have today been given the rare privilege to be host to the nations of the world on our own soil . . .

The time for the healing of the wounds has come.

The moment to bridge the chasms that divide us has come.

The time to build is upon us.

We have, at last, achieved our political emancipation . . .

We have triumphed in the effort to implant hope in the breasts of the millions of our people. We enter into a covenant that we shall build the society in which all South Africans, both black and white, will be able to walk tall, without any fear in their hearts, assured of their inalienable right to human dignity – a rainbow nation at peace with itself and the world . . .

We dedicate this day to all the heroes and heroines in this country and the rest of the world who sacrificed in many ways and surrendered their lives so that we could be free.

Their dreams have become reality. Freedom is their reward.

We understand it still that there is no easy road to freedom.

We know it well that none of us acting alone can achieve success.

We must therefore act together as a united people, for national reconciliation, for nation building, for the birth of a new world.

Let there be justice for all.

Let there be peace for all.

Let there be work, bread, water and salt for all.

Let each know that for each the body, the mind and the soul have been freed to fulfil themselves.

Never, never and never again shall it be that this beautiful land will again experience the oppression of one by another and suffer the indignity of being the skunk of the world.

Let freedom reign.

The sun shall never set on so glorious a human achievement!

God bless Africa!

Thank you.

Winston Churchill, 'We shall fight on the beaches', 4 June 1940

Even Churchill could not have imagined how disastrously the Second World War would go in his first days in office. The Germans rolled through Belgium and Holland and into France, trapping the British army at Dunkirk. He was scarcely exaggerating when he told his Cabinet that 'if this long island story of ours is to end at last, let it end only when each of us lies choking in his own blood upon the ground'. Faced with the downfall of the great land power of France, Churchill knew only the Channel stood between Nazi panzers and a lightly defended Britain. In his second masterpiece of oratory, he delivers this chivalrous poem-speech.

I have, myself, full confidence that if all do their duty, if nothing is neglected, and if best arrangements are made, as they are being made, we shall prove ourselves once again able to defend our island home, to ride out the storm of war, and to outlive the menace of tyranny, if necessary for years, if necessary alone. At any rate, that is what we are going to try to do. That is the resolve of His Majesty's government – every man of them. That is the will of Parliament and the nation. The British Empire and the French Republic, linked together in their cause and in their need, will defend to the death their native soil, aiding each other like good comrades to the utmost of their strength.

Even though large tracts of Europe and many old and famous states have fallen or may fall into the grip of the Gestapo and all the odious apparatus of Nazi rule, we shall not flag or fail. We shall go on to the end, we shall fight in France, we shall fight on the seas and oceans, we shall fight with growing confidence and growing strength in the air, we shall defend our island, whatever the cost may be, we shall fight on the beaches, we shall fight on the landing grounds, we shall fight in the fields and in the streets, we shall fight in the hills; we shall never surrender, and even if, which I do not for a moment believe, this island or a large part of it were subjugated and starving, then our empire beyond the seas, armed and guarded by the British fleet, would carry on the struggle, until, in God's good time, the New World, with all its power and might, steps forth to the rescue and the liberation of the old.

Rise and Fall

Muawiyah, 'When they pull, I loosen', 7th century AD

The best definition of statesmanship and the art of politics. Muawiyah was famous for his personal empathy and political common sense. He personified *hilm*, the wisdom and patience of an Arab sheikh, but he was also the first emperor and monarch of Islam, nicknamed 'Caesar of the Arabs'. Born in 602, he was the son of a powerful aristocrat in pagan Mecca, Abu Sufyan. When the Prophet Mohammed started to preach the new revelation of Islam, his father at first resisted. But when the Prophet's success was clear, Abu Sufyan joined Islam, his daughter married the Prophet and his son Muawiyah became his secretary. Later during the rule of the early Caliphs – successors of the Prophet – the Muslims burst out of the Arabian peninsula and conquered an empire that stretched from North Africa to Persia. At first Muawiyah governed Syria but when his cousin Caliph Othman was assassinated, he fought Mohammed's son-in-law Ali and daughter Fatima in a vicious civil war between those who believed that the Prophet's family were his rightful heirs and those who preferred a more traditional monarchy. In 661, Muawiyah won the war, founding the Ummayad dynasty and moving the capital to Damascus. Adding new provinces to his empire, he ruled as a combination of Arab emperor, channelling the Roman Caesars, and tribal sheikh, like his own forefathers, until his death in 680.

I do not apply my sword where my lash suffices, nor my lash where my tongue is enough. And even if there be one hair binding me to my fellow men, I do not let it break. When they pull, I loosen, and if they loosen, I pull.

Elizabeth I, 'I have reigned with your loves', 30 November 1601

On 30 November 1601, the ageing Queen Elizabeth addressed the House of Commons at her last Parliament. She was sixty-seven, toothless, almost bald and her daily regime of dressing was long and tortuous. Her glory days were long gone. After forty years on the throne, her people muttered about high prices and doubts about the succession – but Elizabeth dazzled her parliamentarians with this last beautiful speech. No unpopular and tarnished politician, royal or not, has ever dealt with discontent so well. Elizabeth died just over a year later.

We have heard your declaration and perceive your care of our estate. I do assure you there is no prince that loves his subjects better, or whose love can countervail our love. There is no jewel, be it of never so rich a price, which I set before this jewel: I mean your love. For I do esteem it more than any treasure or riches; for that we know how to prize, but love and thanks I count invaluable. And, though God hath raised me high, yet this I count the glory of my Crown, that I have reigned with your loves. This makes me that I do not so much rejoice that God hath made me to be a Queen, as to be a Queen over so thankful a people. Therefore I have cause to wish nothing more than to content the subject and that is a duty which I owe. Neither do I desire to live longer days than I may see your prosperity and that is my only desire. And as I am that person still yet, under God, hath delivered you and so I trust by the almighty power of God that I shall be His instrument to preserve you from every peril, dishonour, shame, tyranny and oppression, partly by means of your intended helps which we take very acceptably because it manifesteth the largeness of your good loves and loyalties unto your sovereign.

Of myself I must say this: I never was any greedy, scraping grasper, nor a strait fast-holding Prince, nor yet a waster. My heart was never set on any worldly goods. What you bestow on me, I will not hoard it up, but receive it to bestow on you again. Therefore, render unto them I beseech you Mr Speaker, such thanks as you imagine my heart yieldeth, but my tongue cannot express. Mr Speaker, I would wish you and the rest to stand up for I shall yet trouble you with longer speech. Mr Speaker, you give me thanks but I doubt me I have greater cause to give you thanks, than you me, and I charge you to thank them of the Lower House from me. For had I not received a knowledge from you, I might have fallen into the lapse of an error, only for lack of true information.

. . . I have ever used to set the Last Judgement Day before mine eyes and so to rule as I shall be judged to answer before a higher judge, and now if my kingly bounties have been abused and my grants turned to the hurt of my people contrary to my will and meaning, and if any in authority under me have neglected or perverted what I have committed to them, I hope God will not lay their culps and offences in my charge. I know the title of a King is a glorious title, but assure yourself that the shining glory of princely authority hath not so dazzled the eyes of our understanding, but that we well know and remember that we also are to yield an account of our actions before the great judge. To be a king and wear a crown is a thing more glorious to them that see it than it is pleasant to them that bear it. For myself I was never so much enticed with the glorious name of a King or royal authority of a Queen as delighted that God hath made me his instrument to maintain his truth and glory and to defend his kingdom as I said from peril, dishonour, tyranny and oppression. There will never Queen sit in my seat with more zeal to my country, care to my subjects and that will sooner with willingness venture her life for your good and safety than myself. For it is my desire to live nor reign no longer than my life and reign shall be for your good. And though you have had, and may have, many princes more mighty and wise sitting in this seat, yet you never had nor shall have, any that will be more careful and loving.

Winston Churchill, 'This was their finest hour', 18 June 1940

The war was getting worse and worse. By mid-June 1940, France had negotiated surrender to Hitler, Italy had entered the war as a German ally, and most of Western Europe was under Nazi rule. France was about to fall and Britain was alone. It was for this that Churchill now had to prepare the British people. Here, he turns around the situation to offer not decline and defeat, not just defiance but something transcendent, using quoted speech to look back at this moment and say, 'This was their finest hour.'

We do not yet know what will happen in France or whether the French resistance will be prolonged, both in France and in the French Empire overseas. The French government will be throwing away great opportunities and casting adrift their future if they do not continue the war in accordance with their treaty obligations, from which we have not felt able to release them. The House will have read the historic declaration in which, at the desire of many Frenchmen – and of our own hearts – we have proclaimed our willingness at the darkest hour in French history to conclude a union of common citizenship in this struggle. However matters may go in France or with the French government, or other French governments, we in this island and in the British Empire will never lose our sense of comradeship with the French people. If we are now called upon to endure what they have been suffering, we shall emulate their courage, and if final victory rewards our toils they shall share the gains, aye, and freedom shall be restored to all. We abate nothing of our just demands; not one jot or tittle do we recede. Czechs, Poles, Norwegians, Dutch, Belgians have joined their causes to our own. All these shall be restored.

What General Weygand [the French commander-in-chief] called the Battle of France is over. I expect that the Battle of Britain is about to begin. Upon this battle depends the survival of Christian civilization. Upon it depends our own British life, and the long continuity of our institutions and our empire. The whole fury and might of the enemy must very soon be turned on us.

Hitler knows that he will have to break us in this island or lose the war. If we can stand up to him, all Europe may be free and the life of the world may move forward into broad, sunlit uplands. But if we fail, then the whole world, including the United States, including all that we have known and cared for, will sink into the abyss of a new Dark Age made more sinister, and perhaps more protracted, by the lights of perverted science.

Let us therefore brace ourselves to our duties, and so bear ourselves that if the British Empire and its Commonwealth last for a thousand years, men will still say, 'This was their finest hour.'

Barack Obama, 'America is a place where all things are possible', 4 November 2008

A definition of the idealism of the American experience. It is hard to think of a president who came to power bearing such optimism and hope, ideas that he had harnessed to win the presidency. Born in Hawaii, Obama was the son of a white mother and a black Kenyan father: 'That my father looked nothing like the people around me – that he was black as pitch, my mother white as milk – barely registered in my mind.' His parents divorced, his father returning to Kenya where he was killed in a car crash. His mother married an Indonesian so that he was brought up partly in Jakarta before returning to the United States to attend Harvard Law School where he met his wife Michelle, a fellow lawyer. He was elected to the US Senate in 2005 and possessed a mastery of language and literature which was particularly striking after the clumsiness and inarticulacy of his predecessor. In 2008, elected the first African-American president, and perhaps the best orator since Lincoln, he here defines his American dream.

If there anyone out there who still doubts that America is a place where all things are possible; who still wonders if the dream of our founders is alive in our time; who still questions the power of our democracy, tonight is your answer . . .

And to all those watching tonight from beyond our shores, from parliaments and palaces to those who are huddled around radios in the forgotten corners of our world – our stories are singular, but our destiny is shared, and a new dawn of American leadership is at hand. To those who would tear this world down – we will defeat you. To those who seek peace and security – we support you. And to all those who have wondered if America's beacon still burns as bright – tonight we proved once more that the true strength of our nation comes not from the might of our arms or the scale of our wealth, but from the enduring power of our ideals: democracy, liberty, opportunity, and unyielding hope.

That's the true genius of America: that America can change. Our union can be perfected. What we've already achieved gives us hope for what we can and must achieve tomorrow.

This election had many firsts and many stories that will be told for generations. But one that's on my mind tonight is about a woman who cast her ballot in Atlanta. She's a lot like the millions of others who stood in line to make their voice heard in this election except for one thing: Ann Nixon Cooper is 106 years old.

She was born just a generation past slavery; a time when there were no cars on the road or planes in the sky; when someone like her couldn't vote for two reasons – because she was a woman and because of the color of her skin.

And tonight, I think about all that she's seen throughout her century in America – the heartache and the hope; the struggle and the progress; the times we were told that we can't, and the people who pressed on with that American creed: yes we can.

At a time when women's voices were silenced and their hopes dismissed, she lived to see them stand up and speak out and reach for the ballot. Yes we can.

When there was despair in the dust bowl and depression across the land, she saw a nation conquer fear itself with a New Deal, new jobs and a new sense of common purpose. Yes we can.

When the bombs fell on our Harbor and tyranny threatened the world, she was there to witness a generation rise to greatness and a democracy was saved. Yes we can.

She was there for the buses in Montgomery, the hoses in Birmingham, a bridge in Selma, and a preacher from Atlanta who told a people that 'We Shall Overcome.' Yes we can.

A man touched down on the moon, a wall came down in Berlin, a world was connected by our own science and imagination. And this year, in this election, she touched her finger to a screen, and cast her vote, because after 106 years in America, through the best of times and the darkest of hours, she knows how America can change. Yes we can.

America, we have come so far. We have seen so much. But there is so much more to do. So tonight, let us ask ourselves – if our children should live to see the next century; if my daughters should be so lucky to live as long as Ann Nixon Cooper, what change will they see? What progress will we have made? This is our chance to answer that call. This is our moment. This is our time – to put our people back to work and open doors of opportunity for our kids; to restore prosperity and pro-mote the cause of peace; to reclaim the American Dream and reaffirm that fundamental truth – that out of many, we are one; that while we breathe, we hope, and where we are met with cynicism, and doubt, and those who tell us that we can't, we will respond with that timeless creed that sums up the spirit of a people: Yes We Can.

God bless you, and may God bless the United States of America.

Decency

Abraham Lincoln, 'Until every drop of blood drawn by the lash shall be paid by another drawn with the sword', 4 March 1865

Lincoln's second inaugural address is his finest piece of prose, all the finer for the challenge that he faced in reuniting the Union after four years of bloody war. The Civil War was not yet completed though the victory of the Union was clear. On 8 November 1864, Lincoln was re-elected. But as Lincoln gives his address to the crowd on the Capitol in Washington on 4 March 1865, the fighting is still bitter. This masterpiece must not only heal the wounds of war but also confront the complexity of the reasons for the war and the dark history of slavery in the South. His challenge is how to reconcile the noble enterprise of America as God's country of freedom with its original sin of slavery.

A few weeks later, on 9 April, the South surrendered. Five days later, 14 April, Lincoln attended Ford's Theatre to see the play *Our American Cousin*. Lincoln's bodyguard went for a drink, leaving him unguarded in his box and enabling the Confederate sympathiser John Wilkes Booth, member of a conspiracy to liquidate the entire Unionist leadership, to shoot him in the back of the head.

Fellow countrymen: At this second appearing to take the oath of the presidential office, there is less occasion for an extended address than there was at the first. Then a statement, somewhat in detail, of a course to be pursued, seemed fitting and proper.

Now, at the expiration of four years, during which public declarations have been constantly called forth on every point and phase of the great contest which still absorbs the attention and engrosses the energies of the nation, little that is new could be presented. The progress of our arms, upon which all else chiefly depends, is as well known to the public as to myself; and it is, I trust, reasonably satisfactory and encouraging to all. With high hope for the future, no prediction in regard to it is ventured.

On the occasion corresponding to this four years ago, all thoughts were anxiously directed to an impending civil war. All dreaded it – all sought to avert it. While the inaugural address was being delivered from this place, devoted altogether to saving the Union without war, insurgent agents were in the city seeking to destroy it without war – seeking to dissolve the Union, and divide effects, by negotiation.

Both parties deprecated war; but one of them would make war rather than let the nation survive; and the other would accept war rather than let it perish. And the war came.

One-eighth of the whole population were colored slaves, not distributed generally over the Union, but localized in the Southern part of it. These slaves constituted a peculiar and powerful interest. All knew that this interest was, somehow, the cause of the war. To strengthen, perpetuate, and extend this interest was the object for which the insurgents would rend the Union, even by war; while the government claimed no right to do more than to restrict the territorial enlargement of it.

Neither party expected for the war the magnitude or the duration which it has already attained. Neither anticipated that the cause of the conflict might cease with, or even before, the conflict itself should cease. Each looked for an easier triumph, and a result less fundamental and astounding. Both read the same Bible, and pray to the same God; and each invokes his aid against the other.

It may seem strange that any men should dare to ask a just God's assistance in wringing their bread from the sweat of other men's faces; but let us judge not, that we be not judged. The prayers of both could not be answered – that of neither has been answered fully.

The Almighty has his own purposes. 'Woe unto the world because of offenses! for it must needs be that offenses come; but woe to that man by whom the offense cometh.' If we shall suppose that American slavery is one of those offenses which, in the providence of God, must needs come, but which, having continued through his appointed time, he now wills to remove, and that he gives to both North and South this terrible war, as the woe due to those by whom the offense came, shall we discern therein any departure from those divine attributes which the believers in a living God always ascribe to him? Fondly do we hope – fervently do we pray – that this mighty scourge of war may speedily pass away.

Yet, if God wills that it continue until all the wealth piled by the bondsman's two hundred and fifty years of unrequited toil shall be sunk, and until every drop of blood drawn by the lash shall be paid by another drawn with the sword, as was said three thousand years ago, so still it must be said, 'The judgments of the Lord are true and righteous altogether.' With malice toward none; with charity for all; with firmness in the right, as God gives us to see the right, let us strive on to finish the work we are in; to bind up the nation's wounds; to care for him who shall have borne the battle, and for his widow, and his orphan – to do all which may achieve and cherish a just and lasting peace among ourselves, and with all nations.

John F. Kennedy, 'Ask not what your country can do for you', 20 January 1961

In January 1961, Jack Kennedy, handsome and idealistic, is at forty-three the youngest president ever elected. But there are other sides to him too: his father was the ruthless Wall Street and Hollywood mogul Joe Kennedy, who had shamefully pushed for Britain to negotiate with – in effect surrender to – Hitler while serving as US ambassador to London. The family was already tragic: his father forced one of his siblings to undergo a catastrophic lobotomy while both his eldest brother and elder sister had been killed in plane crashes. Jack himself had had a heroic war, his patrol boat being sunk in the Pacific; he was then elected a senator, before marrying the beautiful socialite Jacqueline Bouvier. The couple exuded glamour – but all was not quite what it seemed. Jack's father's ambition to capture the presidency dominated the family. Jack himself suffered from agonising ailments and was highly medicated but his ill-health was kept secret.

Narrowly beating Republican rival Richard Nixon (supposedly with his father pulling strings, and especially using Mafia help to win Chicago), JFK was determined to create a new style of presidency, promoting the 'best and the brightest' to his cabinet along with his forceful, idealistic brother Bobby as attorney-general. While he would follow a liberal programme he called The New Frontier, cautiously sympathetic to African-American civil rights, he promised to be tough in the Cold War against the USSR. His White House was a family court, later immortalised by Kennedy historians as quasi-mythic, quasi-royal: Camelot.

Using speech writers Ted Sorenson and J. K. Galbraith, Kennedy drafts an inaugural address based on the simplicity of Lincoln's Gettysburg Address. Its most famous rhetorical trick is the chiasmus, the reversal of phrases to achieve telling

emphasis as in the brilliant definition of duty – the heart of
JKF's idealism. Kennedy ruled for just thirty-four months. On
22 November 1963, he was assassinated. This speech is a masterpiece of oratory and ranks with Lincoln's second as the greatest
inaugural address.

Vice-President [Lyndon] Johnson, Mr Speaker, Mr Chief Justice, President Eisenhower, Vice-President Nixon, President Truman, reverend
clergy, fellow citizens:

We observe today not a victory of party but a celebration of freedom,
symbolizing an end as well as a beginning, signifying renewal as well
as change. For I have sworn before you and Almighty God the same
solemn oath our forebears prescribed nearly a century and three-
quarters ago.

The world is very different now. For man holds in his mortal hands
the power to abolish all forms of human poverty and all forms of
human life. And yet the same revolutionary beliefs for which our
forebears fought are still at issue around the globe – the belief that the
rights of man come not from the generosity of the state but from the
hand of God.

We dare not forget today that we are the heirs of that first revolution. Let the word go forth from this time and place, to friend and foe
alike, that the torch has been passed to a new generation of Americans
– born in this century, tempered by war, disciplined by a hard and bitter
peace, proud of our ancient heritage – and unwilling to witness or
permit the slow undoing of those human rights to which this nation
has always been committed, and to which we are committed today at
home and around the world.

Let every nation know, whether it wishes us well or ill, that we shall
pay any price, bear any burden, meet any hardship, support any friend,
oppose any foe to assure the survival and the success of liberty.

This much we pledge – and more . . .

Let us never negotiate out of fear. But let us never fear to negotiate.

Let both sides explore what problems unite us instead of

belabouring those problems which divide us.

Let both sides, for the first time, formulate serious and precise proposals for the inspection and control of arms, and bring the absolute power to destroy other nations under the absolute control of all nations.

Let both sides seek to invoke the wonders of science instead of its terrors. Together let us explore the stars, conquer the deserts, eradicate disease, tap the ocean depths, and encourage the arts and commerce . . .

All this will not be finished in the first one hundred days. Nor will it be finished in the first one thousand days; nor in the life of this Administration; nor even perhaps in our lifetime on this planet. But let us begin.

In your hands, my fellow citizens, more than mine, will rest the final success or failure of our course. Since this country was founded, each generation of Americans has been summoned to give testimony to its national loyalty. The graves of young Americans who answered the call to service surround the globe.

Now the trumpet summons us again – not as a call to bear arms, though arms we need – not as a call to battle, though embattled we are – but a call to bear the burden of a long twilight struggle, year in and year out, rejoicing in hope, patient in tribulation, a struggle against the common enemies of man: tyranny, poverty, disease and war itself.

Can we forge against these enemies a grand and global alliance, North and South, East and West, that can assure a more fruitful life for all mankind? Will you join in that historic effort?

In the long history of the world, only a few generations have been granted the role of defending freedom in its hour of maximum danger. I do not shrink from this responsibility – I welcome it. I do not believe that any of us would exchange places with any other people or any other generation. The energy, the faith, the devotion which we bring to this endeavour will light our country and all who serve it. And the glow from that fire can truly light the world.

And so, my fellow Americans, ask not what your country can do for you; ask what you can do for your country.

My fellow citizens of the world, ask not what America will do for you, but what together we can do for the freedom of man.

Finally, whether you are citizens of America or citizens of the world, ask of us here the same high standards of strength and sacrifice which we ask of you. With a good conscience our only sure reward, with history the final judge of our deeds, let us go forth to lead the land we love, asking His blessing and His help, but knowing that here on earth God's work must truly be our own.

Chimamanda Ngozi Adichie, 'The ability of human beings to make and remake themselves for the better', December 2012

One of the finest novelists of the twenty-first century, Chimamanda Ngozi Adichie was born in Nigeria in 1977 and educated in the US. Her breakthrough novel, *Americanah*, explored those two worlds and how they connect together – but her masterpiece is her earlier, heartbreaking and beautiful novel of love and death in the Biafran War, *Half a Yellow Sun*. Her TED talk about feminism and gender has inspired even more people.

Not long ago, I wrote an article about being young and female in Lagos. And an acquaintance told me that it was an angry article, and I should not have made it so angry. But I was unapologetic. Of course it was angry. Gender as it functions today is a grave injustice. I am angry. We should all be angry. Anger has a long history of bringing about positive change. But I am also hopeful, because I believe deeply in the ability of human beings to remake themselves for the better . . .

We spend too much time teaching girls to worry about what boys think of them. But the reverse is not the case. We don't teach boys to care about being likeable. We spend too much time telling girls they cannot be angry or aggressive or tough, which is bad enough, but then we turn around and either praise or excuse men for the same reasons. All over the world, there are so many magazine articles and books telling women what to do, how to be and not to be, in order to attract or please men. There are far fewer guides for men about pleasing women.

. . . Gender matters everywhere in the world. And I would like today to ask that we should begin to dream about and plan for a different world. A fairer world. A world of happier men and happier women who are truer to themselves. And this is how to start: we must raise our daughters differently. We must also raise our sons differently.

We do a great disservice to boys in how we raise them. We stifle the humanity of boys. We define masculinity in a very narrow way. Masculinity is a hard, small cage, and we put boys inside this cage.

We teach boys to be afraid of fear, of weakness, of vulnerability. We teach them to mask their true selves, because they have to be, in Nigerian-speak, a hard man.

... But by far the worst thing we do to males – by making them feel they have to be hard – is that we leave them with very fragile egos. The harder a man feels compelled to be, the weaker his ego is.

And then we do a much greater disservice to girls, because we raise them to cater to the fragile egos of males.

We teach girls to shrink themselves, to make themselves smaller.

We say to girls, 'You can have ambition, but not too much. You should aim to be successful but not too successful, otherwise you will threaten the man. If you are the breadwinner in your relationship with a man, pretend that you are not, especially in public, otherwise you will emasculate him.'

But what if we question the premise itself? Why should a woman's success be a threat to a man? What if we decide to simply dispose of that word – and I don't know if there is an English word I dislike more than this – emasculation.

A Nigerian acquaintance once asked me if I was worried that men would be intimidated by me.

I was not worried at all – it had not even occurred to me to be worried, because a man who would be intimidated by me is exactly the kind of man I would have no interest in.

Still, I was struck by this. Because I am female, I'm expected to aspire to marriage. I am expected to make my life choices keeping in mind that marriage is the most important. Marriage can be a good thing, a source of joy, love and mutual support. But why do we teach girls to aspire to marriage, yet we don't teach boys the same?

... We raise girls to see each other as competitors – not for jobs or accomplishments, which in my opinion can be a good thing, but for the attention of men.

We teach girls that they cannot be sexual beings in the way boys are.

If we have sons, we don't mind knowing about their girlfriends. But our daughters' boyfriends? God forbid. (But of course we expect them to bring home the perfect man for marriage when the time is right.)

We police girls. We praise girls for virginity but we don't praise boys for virginity (and it makes me wonder how exactly this is supposed to work out, since the loss of virginity is a process that usually involves two people of opposite genders).

. . . We teach girls shame. *Close your legs. Cover yourself.* We make them feel as though by being born female, they are already guilty of something. And so girls grow up to be women who cannot say that they have desire. Who silence themselves. Who cannot say what they truly think. Who have turned pretence into an art form.

. . . The problem with gender is that it prescribes how we should be rather than recognizing how we are. Imagine how much happier we would be, how much freer to our true individual selves, if we didn't have the weight of gender expectations.

Malala Yousafzai, 'One pen and one book can change the world', 12 July 2013

On the evening of 9 October 2012, a bus filled with schoolchildren was stopped by armed men on a remote road in Pakistan. Boarding the bus, they asked, 'Who is Malala?' When they identified which of the schoolgirls was Malala Yousafzai, they shot her in the head and left her for dead. She was young, but already well known in Pakistan as an educational campaigner who believed girls should have the same opportunity to be educated as boys. But a local Islamic fundamentalist Taliban leader banned girls from attending school. Aged only fifteen, Malala bravely opposed him, speaking on television and insisting: 'I didn't want my future to be imprisoned in my four walls and just cooking and giving birth.' Her head wound appeared to be fatal but she was rushed to the military hospital in Peshawar where emergency surgery saved her life and she was later flown to the UK for further treatment. After making a miraculous recovery and having lost none of her courage or articulacy, she was invited to speak to a special youth assembly of the United Nations in New York on her sixteenth birthday, a day the UN called 'Malala Day'. The UN Secretary General, Ban Ki-moon, called her 'our hero'.

In the name of God, the Most Beneficent, the Most Merciful.

Today, it is an honour for me to be speaking again after a long time. Being here with such honourable people is a great moment in my life.

I don't know where to begin my speech. I don't know what people would be expecting me to say. But first of all, thank you to God for whom we all are equal and thank you to every person who has prayed for my fast recovery and a new life. I cannot believe how much love people have shown me.

Dear brothers and sisters, do remember one thing. Malala Day is not my day. Today is the day of every woman, every boy and every girl who have raised their voice for their rights. There are hundreds of human rights activists and social workers who are not only speaking for human rights, but who are struggling to achieve their goals of education, peace and equality. Thousands of people have been killed by the terrorists and millions have been injured. I am just one of them.

So here I stand, one girl among many.

I speak – not for myself, but for all girls and boys.

I raise up my voice – not so that I can shout, but so that those without a voice can be heard.

Those who have fought for their rights.

Their right to live in peace.

Their right to be treated with dignity. Their right to equality of opportunity. Their right to be educated.

Dear friends, on the 9th of October 2012, the Taliban shot me on the left side of my forehead. They shot my friends too. They thought that the bullets would silence us. But they failed. And then, out of that silence, came thousands of voices. The terrorists thought that they would change our aims and stop our ambitions but nothing changed in my life except this: weakness, fear and hopelessness died. Strength, power and courage was born. I am the same Malala. My ambitions are the same. My hopes are the same. My dreams are the same.

Dear sisters and brothers, I am not against anyone. Neither am I here to speak in terms of personal revenge against the Taliban or any other terrorist group. I am here to speak up for the right of education of every child. I want education for the sons and the daughters of all the extremists, especially the Taliban.

I do not even hate the Talib who shot me. Even if there is a gun in my hand and he stands in front of me, I would not shoot him. This is the compassion that I have learned from Mohammed the Prophet of Mercy, Jesus Christ and Lord Buddha. This is the legacy of change that I have inherited from Martin Luther King, Nelson Mandela and Muhammad Ali Jinnah. This is the philosophy of non-violence that I have learned from Gandhi Jee, Bacha Khan and Mother Teresa. And this is the forgiveness that I have learned from my mother and father. This is what my soul is telling me: be peaceful and love everyone.

Dear sisters and brothers, we realize the importance of light when we see darkness. We realize the importance of our voice when we are silenced. In the same way, when we were in Swat, in the north of Pakistan, we realized the importance of pens and books when we saw the guns.

The wise saying 'The pen is mightier than sword' was true. The extremists are afraid of books and pens. The power of education frightens them.

They are afraid of women. The power of the voice of women frightens them. And that is why they killed 14 innocent medical students in the recent attack in Quetta. And that is why they killed many female teachers and polio workers in Khyber Pukhtoon Khwa and FATA. That is why they are blasting schools every day . . .

So let us wage a global struggle against illiteracy, poverty and terrorism, and let us pick up our books and pens. They are our most powerful weapons.

One child, one teacher, one pen and one book can change the world. Education is the only solution. Education First.

Mohandas Gandhi, 'I have faith in the righteousness of our cause', 11 March 1930

Here is the speech that set the tone for Gandhi's campaign to win independence for India. 'Non-violence is the first article of my faith. It is also the last article of my creed,' he said at his trial in 1922 and his embrace of *satyagraha* ('steadfastness in truth') and *ahimsa* ('non-violence') were the pillars of his political career. Born in Gujarat to a poor family, he studied law at the Inner Temple in London before practising law among the Indian community in South Africa where he started campaigning for civil rights, returning to India in 1915.

Then he set about his life's work, to end the British Raj and achieve home rule (*swaraj*) for the multi-racial, multi-religious sub-continent with its huge Hindu and Muslim populations. In 1921 he became leader of the Indian National Congress. On 26 January 1930 he and his fellow leaders demanded total independence, a campaign of civil disobedience spearheaded by a protest against the Salt Taxes (which hit the poor hardest and were widely resented).

After he was arrested in May 1930, Gandhi only intensified his demands. He deliberately eschewed Western suits in favour of traditional Indian clothes, and he fasted and meditated, both to purify himself but also to demonstrate the simplicity and decency of his cause – and his own personal humility. He became India's Mahatma (elevated soul) and Bapu (father). His negotiations with the viceroy infuriated Winston Churchill who denounced him: 'It is alarming and also nauseating to see Mr Gandhi, a seditious Middle Temple lawyer, now posing as a fakir, striding half-naked up the steps of the vice-regal palace . . . to parley on equal terms with the representative of the King-Emperor.' During the Second World War Gandhi attacked Nazism, Communism and British imperialism, telling Indians not to fight for Britain (but many did). At the end of the war, Gandhi opposed India's division along religious lines but was overtaken by the new Muslim nationalism that led to the creation of Hindu India and Muslim Pakistan in August 1947. On 30 January 1948, Gandhi was assassinated by a Hindu nationalist.

Here Gandhi defines his mission on the night before he sets out on his Salt March towards the coast of Gujarat. He fears he might be killed.

In all probability this will be my last speech to you. Even if the government allow me to march tomorrow morning, this will be my last speech on the sacred banks of the Sabarmati. Possibly these may be the last words of my life here.

I have already told you yesterday what I had to say. Today I shall confine myself to what you should do after my companions and I are arrested. The programme of the march to Jalalpur must be fulfilled as originally settled . . .

But let there be not a semblance of breach of peace even after all of us have been arrested. We have resolved to utilize all our resources in the pursuit of an exclusively non-violent struggle. Let no one commit a wrong in anger. This is my hope and prayer. I wish these words of mine reached every nook and corner of the land. My task shall be done if I perish and so do my comrades. It will then be for the Working Committee of the Congress to show you the way and it will be up to you to follow its lead. So long as I have reached Jalalpur, let nothing be done in contravention to the authority vested in me by the Congress. But once I am arrested, the whole responsibility shifts to the Congress. No one who believes in non-violence, as a creed, need, therefore, sit still. My compact with the Congress ends as soon as I am arrested. In that case . . . Wherever possible, civil disobedience of salt [laws] should be started . . .

We are, however, not to be content with this alone. There is no ban by the Congress and wherever the local workers have self-confidence other suitable measures may be adopted. I stress only one condition, namely, let our pledge of truth and non-violence as the only means for the attainment of swaraj be faithfully kept. For the rest, everyone has a free hand . . .

It was the message that I desired to impart to you before starting on the march or for the jail. I wish that there should be no suspension or abandonment of the war that commences tomorrow morning or earlier, if I am arrested before that time. I shall eagerly await the news that ten batches are ready as soon as my batch is arrested. I believe there are men in India to complete the work begun by me. I have faith in the righteousness of our cause and the purity of our weapons. And where the means are clean, God is undoubtedly present with His blessings. And where these three combine, their defeat is an impossibility.

A satyagrahi, whether free or incarcerated, is ever victorious. He is vanquished only when he forsakes truth and non-violence and turns a deaf ear to the inner voice. If, therefore, there is such a thing as defeat for even a satyagrahi, he alone is the cause of it.

God bless you all and keep off all obstacles from the path in the struggle that begins tomorrow.

Susan B. Anthony, 'Are women persons?', February–June 1873

Fearless, resourceful and tough, Susan B. Anthony was an indefatigable campaigner first against slavery, then in favour of temperance and women's suffrage. Born into a Quaker family in 1820, she started campaigning against slavery at the age of seventeen, working for the American Anti Slavery Society. In 1872, Anthony voted in Rochester, New York, and was arrested for illegal voting. She was found guilty. She refused to pay the fine and the trial gave her the chance to launch an intense campaign and lecture tour, of which this speech was a part. In 1878, Anthony and feminist theorist Elizabeth Cady Stanton managed to persuade senators to introduce a constitutional amendment giving women the right to vote. It did not pass, but Anthony never stopped campaigning. She never married, telling those with the temerity to enquire why not: 'I never felt I could give up my life of freedom to become a man's housekeeper. When I was young, if a girl married poor, she became a housekeeper and a drudge. If she married wealth, she became a pet and a doll. Just think, had I married at twenty, I would have been a drudge or a doll for fifty-nine years. Think of it!' But she also reminisced: 'It always happened that the men I wanted were those I could not get, and those who wanted me I wouldn't have.'

Once feared as a threat to society, Anthony became an American hero, invited to the White House by President McKinley on her eightieth birthday. She died in 1906. When the amendment she had proposed in 1878 was passed in 1920, it became the Nineteenth Amendment to the US Constitution, known as the Susan B. Anthony Amendment.

Friends and fellow-citizens: I stand before you tonight, under indictment for the alleged crime of having voted at the last presidential

election, without having a lawful right to vote. It shall be my work this
evening to prove to you that in thus voting, I not only committed no
crime, but, instead, simply exercised my citizen's right, guaranteed to
me and all United States citizens by the National Constitution, beyond
the power of any state to deny.

Our democratic-republican government is based on the idea of the
natural right of every individual member thereof to a voice and a vote
in making and executing the laws. We assert the province of government to be to secure the people in the enjoyment of their unalienable
rights. We throw to the winds the old dogma that governments can
give rights.

. . . Nor can you find a word in any of the grand documents left us by
the [founding] fathers that assumes for government the power to create
or to confer rights. The Declaration of Independence, the United States
Constitution, the constitutions of the several states and the organic
laws of the territories, all alike propose to protect the people in the
exercise of their God-given rights. Not one of them pretends to bestow
rights . . .

One-half of the people of this nation today are utterly powerless to
blot from the statute books an unjust law, or to write there a new and a
just one. The women, dissatisfied as they are with this form of government, that enforces taxation without representation – that compels
them to obey laws to which they have never given their consent, that
imprisons and hangs them without a trial by a jury of their peers, that
robs them, in marriage, of the custody of their own persons, wages
and children – are this half of the people left wholly at the mercy of the
other half, in direct violation of the spirit and letter of the declarations
of the framers of this government, every one of which was based on the
immutable principle of equal rights to all . . .?

It was we, the people, not we, the white male citizens, nor yet we, the
male citizens; but we, the whole people, who formed this Union. And
we formed it, not to give the blessings or liberty, but to secure them;
not to the half of ourselves and the half of our posterity, but to the
whole people – women as well as men. And it is downright mockery to

talk to women of their enjoyment of the blessings of liberty while they are denied the use of the only means of securing them provided by this democratic-republican government – the ballot.

. . . For any state to make sex a qualification that must ever result in the disfranchisement of one entire half of the people, is to pass a bill of attainder, or an *ex post facto* law, and is therefore a violation of the supreme law of the land. By it, the blessings of liberty are forever withheld from women and their female posterity. To them, this government has no just powers derived from the consent of the governed. To them this government is not a democracy. It is not a republic. It is an odious aristocracy; a hateful oligarchy of sex. The most hateful aristocracy ever established on the face of the globe . . . this oligarchy of sex, which makes father, brothers, husband, sons, the oligarchs over the mother and sisters, the wife and daughters of every household; which ordains all men sovereigns, all women subjects, carries dissension, discord and rebellion into every home of the nation . . .

The only question left to be settled, now, is: Are women persons? And I hardly believe any of our opponents will have the hardihood to say they are not. Being persons, then, women are citizens, and no state has a right to make any new law, or to enforce any old law, that shall abridge their privileges or immunities. Hence, every discrimination against women in the constitutions and laws of the several states, is today null and void, precisely as is every one against negroes . . .

Elizabeth II, 'We will be with our friends; we will be with our families; we will meet again', 5 April 2020

The global crisis of the COVID-19 pandemic saw bewildered governments unsure how to cope with a new and mysterious disease, bemused by confusingly different scientific views, their leaders unable to deliver any inspiring oratory. Instead it was the British Queen, aged ninety-three and known for her austere sense of duty, who in a simple yet powerful speech perfectly expressed the spirit of the time. It boasts fine ideas especially relevant to the British dilemma – 'The pride in who we are is not a part of our past, it defines our present and our future' – but even better was the three-note rhythm in the penultimate sentence that echoed and restored the famous wartime song 'We'll Meet Again . . .'

I am speaking to you at what I know is an increasingly challenging time.

A time of disruption in the life of our country; a disruption that has brought grief to some, financial difficulties to many, and enormous changes to the daily lives of us all.

I want to thank everyone on the NHS frontline, as well as care workers and those carrying out essential roles, who selflessly continue their day-to-day duties outside the home in support of us all.

I am sure the nation will join me in assuring you that what you do is appreciated and every hour of your hard work brings us closer to a return to more normal times.

I also want to thank those of you who are staying at home, thereby helping to protect the vulnerable and sparing many families the pain already felt by those who have lost loved ones.

Together we are tackling this disease, and I want to reassure you that if we remain united and resolute, then we will overcome it.

I hope in the years to come everyone will be able to take pride in how they responded to this challenge.

And those who come after us will say the Britons of this generation were as strong as any.

That the attributes of self-discipline, of quiet good-humoured resolve and of fellow feeling still characterise this country.

The pride in who we are is not a part of our past, it defines our present and our future.

The moments when the United Kingdom has come together to applaud its care and essential workers will be remembered as an expression of our national spirit; and its symbol will be the rainbows drawn by children.

And though self-isolating may at times be hard, many people of all faiths, and of none, are discovering that it presents an opportunity to slow down, pause and reflect, in prayer or meditation.

It reminds me of the very first broadcast I made, in 1940, helped by my sister.

We, as children, spoke from here at Windsor to children who had been evacuated from their homes and sent away for their own safety.

Today, once again, many will feel a painful sense of separation from their loved ones. But now, as then, we know, deep down, that it is the right thing to do.

While we have faced challenges before, this one is different.

This time we join with all nations across the globe in a common endeavour, using the great advances of science and our instinctive compassion to heal.

We will succeed – and that success will belong to every one of us.

We should take comfort that while we may have more still to endure, better days will return: we will be with our friends again; we will be with our families again; we will meet again.

But for now, I send my thanks and warmest good wishes to you all.

Battlefields

George S. Patton, Jr, 'I am personally going to shoot that paper-hanging sonofabitch Hitler', 5 June 1944

Here's a soldier's speech about war. Bloody-minded, brutal, and profane, here the quintessential American fighting general – George 'Blood & Guts' Patton – prepares his ordinary infantrymen for the killing and death in battle during the D-Day Allied invasion of Nazi-occupied Europe. 'Paper-hanging' seems to refer to Hitler's supposed early employment as a painter/decorator – though painting postcards was his actual career.

. . . You are here today for three reasons. First, because you are here to defend your homes and your loved ones. Second, you are here for your own self-respect, because you would not want to be anywhere else. Third, you are here because you are real men and all real men like to fight. When you, here, every one of you, were kids, you all admired the champion marble player, the fastest runner, the toughest boxer, the big-league ball players, and the All-American football players. Americans love a winner.

Americans will not tolerate a loser. Americans despise cowards. Americans play to win all of the time. I wouldn't give a hoot in hell for a man who lost and laughed. That's why Americans have never lost nor will ever lose a war; for the very idea of losing is hateful to an American.

You are not all going to die. Only two per cent of you right here today would die in a major battle. Death must not be feared. Death, in time, comes to all men. Yes, every man is scared in his first battle. If he says he's not, he's a liar. Some men are cowards but they fight the same as the brave men or they get the hell slammed out of them watching men fight who are just as scared as they are.

The real hero is the man who fights even though he is scared. Some men get over their fright in a minute under fire. For some, it takes an hour.

For some it takes days. But a real man will never let his fear of death overpower his honour, his sense of duty to his country and his innate manhood.

Battle is the most magnificent competition in which a human being can indulge. It brings out all that is best and removes all that is base. Americans pride themselves on being He Men and they are He Men.

Remember that the enemy is just as frightened as you are, and probably more so. They are not supermen.

. . . All of the real heroes are not storybook combat fighters, either. Every single man in this army plays a vital role. Don't ever let up. Don't ever think that your job is unimportant. Every man has a job to do and he must do it. Every man is a vital link in the great chain. What if every truck driver suddenly decided that he didn't like the whine of those shells overhead, turned yellow, and jumped headlong into a ditch? The cowardly bastard could say, 'Hell, they won't miss me, just one man in thousands.' But, what if every man thought that way? Where in the hell would we be now? What would our country, our loved ones, our homes, even the world, be like? No, goddamnit, Americans don't think like that. Every man does his job. Every man serves the whole. Every department, every unit, is important in the vast scheme of this war.

. . . Sure, we want to go home. We want this war over with. The quickest way to get it over with is to go get the bastards who started it. The quicker they are whipped, the quicker we can go home. The shortest way home is through Berlin and Tokyo. And when we get to Berlin, I am personally going to shoot that paper-hanging sonofabitch Hitler. Just like I'd shoot a snake!

. . . There is one great thing that you men will all be able to say after this war is over and you are home once again. You may be thankful that twenty years from now when you are sitting by the fireplace with your grandson on your knee and he asks you what you did in the great World War II, you won't have to cough, shift him to the other knee and say, 'Well, your granddaddy shovelled shit in Louisiana.' No, sir, you can look him straight in the eye and say, 'Son, your granddaddy rode with the great Third Army and a son-of-a-goddamned-bitch named Georgie Patton!'

Alexander the Great, 'You have Alexander', November 333 BC

The conquest of the known world is the prize. The conquerors are Alexander and his Macedonian army. The target is the Persian empire. Alexander's 40,000 men confront perhaps 100,000 under the command of the Great King Darius II. As the two armies face each other at Issus in Anatolia on 5 November 333 BC, Alexander speaks. His father Philip II of Macedonia had trained a superb army using new tactics and dominated Greece but he had been assassinated before he could begin his dream campaign: the conquest of the ancestral Greek enemy, Persia. Alexander, who may have conspired in his own father's murder, inherited the throne at nineteen years old. Romanticised by historians after his early death, he was a rough soldier, brilliant general, heavy drinker, ruthless and paranoid politician – but he was also highly educated by Aristotle and fascinated by other cultures. Even though his speeches are recounted by historians such as Arrian and Curtius Rufinus long after his death, he was clearly a fine orator too and the essence of his words was recorded. After this speech, Alexander won the battle of Issus, though Darius escaped to fight one more battle which he also lost. By the age of twenty-five Alexander ruled from the Adriatic to the Indus. When he died aged thirty-two, his empire broke up. Has any leader ever defined his own supremacy so neatly as this: 'You have Alexander; they – Darius!'

Remember, that already danger has often threatened you and you have looked it triumphantly in the face; this time the struggle will be between a victorious army and an enemy already once vanquished. God himself, moreover, by suggesting to Darius to leave the open ground and cram his great army into a confined space, has taken charge of operations in our behalf. We ourselves shall have room enough to deploy our infantry, while they, no match for us either in bodily strength or resolution, will find their superiority in numbers of no avail. Our enemies are Medes and Persians, men who for centuries have lived soft and luxurious lives; we of Macedon for generations past have been trained in the hard school of danger and war. Above all, we are free men, and they are slaves. There are Greek troops, to be sure, in Persian service – but how different is their cause from ours! They will be fighting for pay – and not much of it at that; we, on the contrary, shall fight for Greece, and our hearts will be in it. As for our foreign troops – Thracians, Paeonians, Illyrians, Agrianes – they are the best and stoutest soldiers in Europe, and they will find as their opponents the slackest and softest of the tribes of Asia. And what, finally, of the two men in supreme command? You have Alexander – they, Darius!

George W. Bush, 'Today, our nation saw evil', 11 September 2001

Sitting in a school, reading children's stories, President George W. Bush learned that the United States was under attack by hijacked airliners full of people, piloted by fanatic jihadi terrorists and transformed into flying bombs. After a disputed election that almost lost him the White House, Bush, a bluff, cheerful former alcoholic turned Christian evangelical with the air of an insouciant fratboy, son of the 41st president, had served as Governor of Texas but unlike other presidents faced with world crises, such as FDR and JFK, he knew little of the world. When the nineteen hijackers flew three planes into the towers of the World Trade Center and the Pentagon (while in the fourth, heroic passengers fought the terrorists who crashed the plane), 2,996 were killed, a number similar to Pearl Harbor. Bush learned that an Islamic Sunni terrorist, a Saudi named Osama bin Laden, founder of an organisation called al-Qaeda, had ordered this attack from his secret bases in Afghanistan where he was protected by its Taliban rulers.

On the evening of the attacks, as fear, anger and paranoia swept the country, the inarticulate and clumsy Bush addresses the American people. It is not a great speech, but it launches a new era, that of the Global War on Terrorism. Bush ordered invasions of first Afghanistan and then Iraq, believing its dictator Saddam Hussein was somehow linked to al-Qaeda and was developing weapons of mass destruction. No such weapons were found, Saddam was not linked to al-Qaeda, and after an initial success, the country was almost overrun first by a merciless Islamist uprising and then by so-called Islamic State. Half a million civilians and over 4,000 US troops died before a tenuous peace and a flawed democracy were established.

Good evening.

Today, our fellow citizens, our way of life, our very freedom came under attack in a series of deliberate and deadly terrorist acts. The victims were in airplanes or in their offices: secretaries, businessmen and women, military and federal workers, moms and dads, friends and neighbors.

Thousands of lives were suddenly ended by evil, despicable acts of terror. The pictures of airplanes flying into buildings, fires burning, huge structures collapsing have filled us with disbelief, terrible sadness and a quiet, unyielding anger. These acts of mass murder were intended to frighten our nation into chaos and retreat. But they have failed. Our country is strong.

A great people has been moved to defend a great nation. Terrorist attacks can shake the foundations of our biggest buildings, but they cannot touch the foundation of America. These acts shatter steel, but they cannot dent the steel of American resolve. America was targeted for attack because we're the brightest beacon for freedom and opportunity in the world. And no one will keep that light from shining. Today, our nation saw evil – the very worst of human nature – and we responded with the best of America.

With the daring of our rescue workers, with the caring for strangers and neighbors who came to give blood and help in any way they could . . .

The search is underway for those who were behind these evil acts. I have directed the full resources of our intelligence and law enforcement communities to find those responsible and to bring them to justice. We will make no distinction between the terrorists who committed these acts and those who harbor them.

. . . America and our friends and allies join with all those who want peace and security in the world, and we stand together to win the war against terrorism.

. . . This is a day when all Americans from every walk of life unite in our resolve for justice and peace. America has stood down enemies before, and we will do so this time. None of us will ever forget this day, yet we go forward to defend freedom and all that is good and just in our world.

Thank you. Good night. And God bless America.

Tim Collins, 'Tread lightly there', 19 March 2003

As the American and British armies muster to invade Iraq in 2003, a British officer addresses his troops with a laconic humanity. Colonel Tim Collins gives this pep talk to the 1st Battalion of the Royal Irish Regiment in Iraq, one of the best pre-battle talks of modern times.

We go to liberate, not to conquer.

We will not fly our flags in their country. We are entering Iraq to free a people and the only flag which will be flown in that ancient land is their own.

Show respect for them.

There are some who are alive at this moment who will not be alive shortly.

Those who do not wish to go on that journey, we will not send.

As for the others, I expect you to rock their world.

Wipe them out if that is what they choose.

But if you are ferocious in battle remember to be magnanimous in victory.

Iraq is steeped in history.

It is the site of the Garden of Eden, of the Great Flood and the birthplace of Abraham.

Tread lightly there.

You will see things that no man could pay to see – and you will have to go a long way to find a more decent, generous and upright people than the Iraqis.

You will be embarrassed by their hospitality even though they have nothing.

Don't treat them as refugees for they are in their own country.

Their children will be poor, in years to come they will know that the light of liberation in their lives was brought by you.

If there are casualties of war then remember that when they woke up and got dressed in the morning they did not plan to die this day.

Allow them dignity in death.

Bury them properly and mark their graves.

It is my foremost intention to bring every single one of you out alive.

But there may be people among us who will not see the end of this campaign.

We will put them in their sleeping bags and send them back.

There will be no time for sorrow.

The enemy should be in no doubt that we are his nemesis and that we are bringing about his rightful destruction.

There are many regional commanders who have stains on their souls and they are stoking the fires of hell for Saddam.

He and his forces will be destroyed by this coalition for what they have done.

As they die they will know their deeds have brought them to this place. Show them no pity.

It is a big step to take another human life.

It is not to be done lightly.

I know of men who have taken life needlessly in other conflicts.

I can assure you they live with the mark of Cain upon them.

If someone surrenders to you then remember they have that right in international law and ensure that one day they go home to their family.

The ones who wish to fight, well, we aim to please.

If you harm the regiment or its history by over-enthusiasm in killing or in cowardice, know it is your family who will suffer.

You will be shunned unless your conduct is of the highest – for your deeds will follow you down through history.

We will bring shame on neither our uniform or our nation.

It is not a question of if, it's a question of when.

We know he has already devolved the decision to lower command-ers, and that means he has already taken the decision himself.

If we survive the first strike we will survive the attack.

As for ourselves, let's bring everyone home and leave Iraq a better place for us having been there.

Our business now is North.

Franklin D. Roosevelt, 'A date which will live in infamy', 8 December 1941

Roosevelt was in his third term as president, already unprecedented. Between 1939 and 1941, he tried to support beleaguered Britain, the democracy that shared so many American values as it struggled to survive in a Europe that was completely dominated by the brutish power of Hitler's Nazism. In his own country, he faced a strong isolationist movement for America First that contained elements of Fascism and antisemitism. By mid-1941, the Japanese Empire had a decision to make: either to strike west to join Hitler's invasion of Russia – or east against America and the British colonies in the Far East. On 7 December, without warning, the Japanese attacked America, bombing Pearl Harbor, the naval base in Hawaii, sinking eight battleships and killing 2,403. Japan hoped to pre-empt any American containment as they conquered the East but it had the opposite effect. This is FDR's reaction. Stalin and Molotov had used very similar phrases to FDR's 'day of infamy' to describe Hitler's invasion of Russia earlier that year. The phrase is not original but it works.

Mr Vice President, Mr Speaker, members of the Senate, and of the House of Representatives:

Yesterday, December 7th, 1941 – a date which will live in infamy – the United States of America was suddenly and deliberately attacked by naval and air forces of the Empire of Japan.

The United States was at peace with that nation and, at the solicitation of Japan, was still in conversation with its government and its emperor looking toward the maintenance of peace in the Pacific. Indeed, one hour after Japanese air squadrons had commenced bombing in the American island of Oahu, the Japanese Ambassador to the United States and his colleagues delivered to our Secretary of State a formal reply to a recent American message. And while this reply stated that it seemed useless to continue the existing diplomatic negotiations, it contained no threat or hint of war or of armed attack.

It will be recorded that the distance of Hawaii from Japan makes it obvious that the attack was deliberately planned many days or even weeks ago . . .

The attack yesterday on the Hawaiian islands has caused severe damage to American naval and military forces. I regret to tell you that very many American lives have been lost. In addition, American ships have been reported torpedoed on the high seas between San Francisco and Honolulu.

Yesterday, the Japanese government also launched an attack against Malaya. Last night, Japanese forces attacked [the British colony of] Hong Kong. Last night, Japanese forces attacked [US possessions] Guam . . . the Philippine Islands . . . Wake Island . . . Midway Island.

Japan has, therefore, undertaken a surprise offensive extending throughout the Pacific area. The facts of yesterday and today speak for themselves.

The people of the United States have already formed their opinions and well understand the implications to the very life and safety of our nation.

As commander-in-chief of the army and navy, I have directed that all measures be taken for our defense. But always will our whole nation remember the character of the onslaught against us.

No matter how long it may take us to overcome this premeditated invasion, the American people in their righteous might will win through to absolute victory.

I believe that I interpret the will of the Congress and of the people when I assert that we will not only defend ourselves to the uttermost, but will make it very certain that this form of treachery shall never again endanger us.

Hostilities exist. There is no blinking at the fact that our people, our territory, and our interests are in grave danger.

With confidence in our armed forces, with the unbounding

determination of our people, we will gain the inevitable triumph – so help us God.

I ask that the Congress declare that since the unprovoked and dastardly attack by Japan on Sunday, December 7th, 1941, a state of war has existed between the United States and the Japanese Empire.

Defiance

Cleopatra, 'I will not be triumphed over', 30 BC

The shortest and clearest speech in this anthology. Its laconic force reflects the personality of its deliverer: a proud woman in defeat deciding her own fate. A queen of the grandest dynasty of the ancient world, Cleopatra was descended from Ptolemy I, general and cousin of Alexander the Great, who founded his own kingdom in Egypt after the death of the great conqueror in 324 BC. Almost three centuries later, Cleopatra, who was almost completely Greek by blood, was born in 69 BC to a decadent, ruthless and decaying dynasty that was struggling to control its realm, faced with the rise of Rome. Succeeding to the throne, ruling, as was tradition, with her brother-husband, she was a merciless politician, ultimately killing two of her brothers and one of her sisters.

It is ironic she has become a feminist icon because her entire career was based on her realisation that the only way to save her kingdom was through sexual alliances with male potentates. She was twenty-one and fighting a civil war against her brother when she met Roman dictator Julius Caesar who was in his forties. Gifted in political theatre, she had herself delivered to Caesar's presence in a rolled-up carpet. Caesar backed her in the war, restored her rule and fathered her son, Caesarion, who would rule with her. When Caesar was assassinated in 44, she became the lover of Caesar's cavalry general Mark Antony, who split the empire with Caesar's heir and great-nephew, Octavian (the future Emperor Augustus). Antony ruled the east, embracing a Hellenistic lifestyle, adding to Cleopatra's kingdoms and promising future crowns to their three children, all of which offended the Romans.

When a civil war starts in 31, Octavian defeats Antony and Cleopatra at Actium and they flee back to Alexandria where Antony commits suicide. Octavian pursues them. Cleopatra

receives him in a frosty interview. He offers to spare her life and
compliments her imperious dignity but she realises he wishes
to display her in his victory parade. Hence, in a rare quotation
of her actual words, she declares her defiance repeatedly to the
victor. Her declaration has two meanings: not only will she not
be led in a Roman truimph, she will not be triumphed over as a
woman. As soon as he is gone, she kills herself with the venom
of a snake – or at least, by poison.

I will not be triumphed over.

Oliver Cromwell, 'In the name of God, go!', 20 April 1653

Never has political exasperation been expressed with such irascible intemperance as this speech by Oliver Cromwell in his dismissal of an obstructive Parliament. Cromwell had been an obscure country gentleman and Member of Parliament until the confrontation began between King Charles I and the English Parliament, sparking a civil war. Cromwell, who had no military experience, raised a corps of cavalry and gradually emerged as a superb military commander, creating a New Model Army that defeated the royal army, winning the war – and emerging as chief of a military junta. He was highly religious, leaning towards the Puritan side of Protestantism, but politically and socially conservative. Leading his men into battle singing hymns, he never doubted that he was doing God's work, however bloody. He agreed to the trial and execution of Charles I. Cromwell massacred Catholics in Ireland, then defeated a Scottish invasion. He struggled to control both the conservative ruling class and the ever more extreme radicals. Parliament had been purged in December 1649 but even its sixty-man Rump proved obstructive. Now on 20 April 1653, his patience snaps in what sounds like a spontaneous outburst. The final order – 'In the name of God, go!' – was also used against Prime Minister Neville Chamberlain in May 1940, shortly before his downfall. Cromwell ruled Britain as Lord Protector until his death in 1658.

It is high time for me to put an end to your sitting in this place, which you have dishonoured by your contempt of all virtue, and defiled by your practice of every vice; ye are a factious crew, and enemies to all good government; ye are a pack of mercenary wretches, and would like Esau sell your country for a mess of potage, and like Judas betray your

God for a few pieces of money; is there a single virtue now remaining amongst you? Is there one vice you do not possess? Ye have no more religion than my horse; gold is your God; which of you have not bar-ter'd your conscience for bribes? Is there a man amongst you that has the least care for the good of the Commonwealth? Ye sordid prostitutes have you not defil'd this sacred place, and turn'd the Lord's temple into a den of thieves, by your immoral principles and wicked practices? Ye are grown intolerably odious to the whole nation; you were deputed here by the people to get grievances redress'd, are yourselves become the greatest grievance. Your country therefore calls upon me to cleanse this Augean stable, by putting a final period to your iniquitous proceed-ings in this House; and which by God's help, and the strength he has given me, I am now come to do; I command ye therefore, upon the peril of your lives, to depart immediately out of this place; go, get you out! Make haste! Ye venal slaves be gone! Go! Take away that shining bauble there, and lock up the doors. In the name of God, go!

Ronald Reagan, 'Mr Gorbachev, tear down this wall!', 12 June 1987

When Reagan was elected President in 1981, his earlier career as an actor suggested he lacked gravitas, but his career in politics was longer than his time in movies and he had served as Governor of California. Breezy, sunny, witty and easy-going, he had a clear view of what he wanted to achieve in politics. Reagan promised a new age of optimism expressed in one of his election advertisements as 'morning in America'. Early in his term, he was shot and almost killed but when he woke up, he told his wife Nancy, 'Sorry honey, I forgot to duck.' When in a presidential debate his opponent cited his age, he replied, 'I want you to know that also I will not make age an issue of this campaign. I am not going to exploit, for political purposes, my opponent's youth and inexperience.' When he was accused of being lazy, he quipped, 'It's true that hard work never killed anybody. But why take the chance?'

Abroad, Reagan was convinced that the Soviet Union was an 'evil empire' that was not only repressive and aggressive but also vulnerable and decrepit. In this, as in many other things, Reagan's instincts were more accurate than many foreign policy experts. Visiting the Brandenburg Gate in Berlin, where the barbed wire and snipers on the Berlin Wall imprisoned the East Germans within a Communist state, Reagan was determined to challenge the Soviet leader Gorbachev and channel John F. Kennedy's *Ich bin ein Berliner* speech. His advisors counselled against this brazen rhetoric but his speechwriter Peter Robinson was inspired by a conversation with a young German who suggested its key line. Two years later, popular revolts undermined Soviet rule and Gorbachev, reforming and liberalising life within the Soviet Union, allowed Berliners and eastern Europeans to free themselves of Communist rule. They tore down the wall.

Twenty-four years ago, President John F. Kennedy visited Berlin, speaking to the people of this city and the world at the City Hall. Well, since then two other presidents have come, each in his turn, to Berlin. And today I, myself, make my second visit to your city. We come to Berlin, we American Presidents, because it's our duty to speak, in this place, of freedom. But I must confess, we're drawn here by other things as well: by the feeling of history in this city, more than 500 years older than our own nation; by the beauty of the Grunewald and the Tiergarten; most of all, by your courage and determination. Perhaps the composer Paul Lincke understood something about American Presidents. You see, like so many presidents before me, I come here today because wherever I go, whatever I do, *Ich hab noch einen Koffer in Berlin*, I still have a suitcase in Berlin.

. . . Behind me stands a wall that encircles the free sectors of this city, part of a vast system of barriers that divides the entire continent of Europe.

From the Baltic, south, those barriers cut across Germany in a gash of barbed wire, concrete, dog runs, and guard towers. Farther south, there may be no visible, no obvious wall. But there remain armed guards and checkpoints all the same – still a restriction on the right to travel, still an instrument to impose upon ordinary men and women the will of a totalitarian state. Yet it is here in Berlin where the wall emerges most clearly; here, cutting across your city, where the news photo and the television screen have imprinted this brutal division of a continent upon the mind of the world. Standing before the Brandenburg Gate, every man is a German, separated from his fellow men. Every man is a Berliner, forced to look upon a scar.

[. . .]

In the 1950s, Khrushchev predicted: 'We will bury you.' But in the West today, we see a free world that has achieved a level of prosperity and well-being unprecedented in all human history. In the communist world, we see failure, technological backwardness, declining standards of health, even want of the most basic kind – too little food. Even today, the Soviet Union still cannot feed itself. After these four decades, then, there stands before the entire world one great and inescapable conclusion: Freedom leads to prosperity. Freedom replaces the ancient hatreds among the nations with comity and peace. Freedom is the victor.

And now the Soviets themselves may, in a limited way, be coming to understand the importance of freedom . . .

There is one sign the Soviets can make that would be unmistakeable, that would advance dramatically the cause of freedom and peace. General Secretary Gorbachev, if you seek peace, if you seek prosperity for the Soviet Union and Eastern Europe, if you seek liberalization: come here to this gate! Mr Gorbachev, open this gate! Mr Gorbachev, tear down this wall!

. . . As I looked out a moment ago from the Reichstag, that embodiment of German unity, I noticed words crudely spray-painted upon the wall, perhaps by a young Berliner: 'This wall will fall. Beliefs become reality.' Yes, across Europe, this wall will fall. For it cannot withstand faith; it cannot withstand truth. The wall cannot withstand freedom.

Thank you and God bless you all.

Winston Churchill, 'The Few', 20 August 1940

As Hitler's air war against Britain reached its climax Winston Churchill, in his fourth oratorical masterpiece of that desperate and extraordinary year, praises the young pilots of the Royal Air Force who are giving their lives to save the country from Nazi invasion in the so-called Battle of Britain.

The gratitude of every home in our Island, in our Empire, and indeed throughout the world, except in the abodes of the guilty, goes out to the British airmen who, undaunted by odds, unwearied in their constant challenge and mortal danger, are turning the tide of the World War by their prowess and by their devotion. Never in the field of human conflict was so much owed by so many to so few. All hearts go out to the fighter pilots, whose brilliant actions we see with our own eyes day after day . . .

Terror

Al-Hajjaj ibn Yusuf, 'By God I'll grind you down to dust', Kufa, Iraq, AD 694

The eloquence of terror. This sermon, famed for its poetical rhythms, pungent malice and flint-hearted fury, was delivered by al-Hajjaj, a former Arabian schoolteacher who had become the chief henchman and enforcer of the Umayyad Caliph Abd al-Malik. Appointed to govern the rebellious province of Iraq, he spoke at Friday prayers to the people of Kufa, as his troops surrounded the town. After the sermon, he unleashed his soldiers on the people, ordering them to murder anyone who showed the slightest defiance. Thousands were killed.

Oh, people of Kufa! By God I can bear the weight of evil, grab it like a shoe by its sole, and strike them with it. I see hungry stares and straining necks, I see ripened heads ready to be plucked; I am their master. I see blood flowing between turbans and beards . . .

Oh, people of Iraq, centre of disunity, hypocrisy, corruption and vice, I have been chosen for my experience.

The Commander of the Faithful, Abd al-Malik ibn Marwan – may God prolong his life – gathered his arrows, loaded his bow, then struck you with the arrow that is me, because you succumbed to temptation, got swept away by delusion and walked the road of darkness . . .

By God I'll grind you down to dust, and beat you like unruly camels. I never promise without delivering, I never act without finishing.

The Commander of the Faithful instructed me to offer you your due and direct you to fight the enemy, the enemy of our leader. Know that I have taken a solemn oath to God that anyone who betrays this command, after taking his dues, will be swiftly beheaded and pillaged.

Nikolai Yezhov, Josef Stalin and others, 'These swine must be strangled', 4 December 1936

The terrifying witch-hunting speech that intensifies Stalin's Great Terror, in which a million innocent people were executed for crimes they did not commit.

Stalin was a Georgian cobbler's son who embraced Marxism as a teenager. After serving many terms of exile and prison as a professional revolutionary, he helped Lenin seize power in October 1917 and became one of the leaders in the tiny clique of Bolsheviks that ruled Soviet Russia. When Lenin died, Stalin emerged as his successor, defeating more famous luminaries such as Trotsky, Zinoviev and Bukharin to become dictator. But his ruthless policies of collectivisation and industrialisation revealed disloyalty among the Bolshevik leaders. In December 1934, his ally Kirov was assassinated. Stalin exploited the crisis to organise a reckoning with his enemies – or anyone who might threaten his power in the coming war against Hitler. To do so, he promoted a trusted young Bolshevik named Nikolai Yezhov to lead a campaign of denunciation and hate that systematically framed Stalin's enemies as members of a secretive, pervasive conspiracy to kill Stalin and betray the revolution. The evidence was procured by the secret police who tortured victims into giving false testimony. Yezhov first organised the trial and execution of Zinoviev.

Now in December 1936, at the secret Plenum of the ruling Central Committee, Yezhov, the newly promoted People's Commissar for Internal Affairs (NKVD), attacks another leader, Bukharin, who had once been Stalin's closest ally. Stalin backs Yezhov up. Other leaders, keen to rise to power, or terrified of being implicated themselves, join in shouting 'The swine!' and 'The brutes!' In the opening weeks and months of 1937, many of the leadership were arrested and killed before

Stalin called a halt in 1938 – when Yezhov himself was arrested and shot.

YEZHOV: . . . You know that already at the August trial Zinoviev testified that apart from the main centre of the Zinovievist-Trotskyist bloc, there existed also a backup centre. Zinoviev gave four surnames as members of the backup centre: Piatakov, Sokolnikov, Radek and Serebriakov. All four members of the backup centre have testified that they were members of the centre . . .

I must say that this so-called backup centre, despite the fact that, according to the original testimony of Piatakov, had become active only after the collapse of the main centre – that is, after the arrest of Zinoviev, Kamenev, Smirnov, and others – despite this, it had deployed its activities significantly earlier, especially Piatakov. At any rate, the activity of this centre was significantly more dangerous, if one may so express oneself, or more filthy, even in comparison with the counter-revolutionary work of the previous centre that had been exposed. To a certain degree, this is explained by the fact that it had the opportunity to work in a more clandestine manner, that it had a more clandestine means of carrying on its work, that it had elicited greater trust to it, so it deployed its activities to a significantly greater degree. At any rate, if we look at it in terms of its connections, it enjoyed significantly greater connections with the periphery than did the centre whose trial took place in 1936.

BERIA: And also in terms of its connections abroad.

YEZHOV: Yes, that's true.

YEZHOV: As for the ties linking the so-called backup centre and the periphery, they were strong, whether we speak of personal ties or ties with groups of people . . .

In the Azov–Black Sea organisation over 200 persons, headed by Glebov, Beloborodov, and others, were arrested. In Georgia over 300 persons headed by Akudzhava were arrested. In Leningrad over 400 persons and in Sverdlovsk over 100 persons were arrested.

We should add that the rather large group of Trotskyists in Sverdlovsk was in fact directed by Japanese intelligence through Kniazev, formerly head of Japanese intelligence [in Sverdlovsk] ...

At any rate, people not only discussed the question of terror, they also concretely prepared for it. At any rate, many attempts were made to carry out terrorist acts of assassination. In particular, the Azov–Black Sea counter-revolutionary terrorist group headed by Beloborodov assigned a group under the direction of a certain Dukat from the Trotskyists, who tried to hunt down Comrade Stalin in Sochi. Beloborodov gave instructions to Dukat so that the latter could take advantage of Comrade Stalin's stay in Sochi on his vacation, so that he could find a propitious moment to carry out his assassination. When Dukat failed in his attempt, Beloborodov vilified him in every way possible for failing to organise this business ...

Here is an example of the most vivid testimony from that region, testimony given by Norkin, now under arrest ... he reports about Piatakov's attitude to the workers at the time he gave them their subversive assignments: 'At his last meeting, in July 1936, Piatakov said, "So, I see you've found someone to pity, haven't you, that herd of sheep—"'

BERIA: The swine! [Noise of indignation in the room]

A VOICE: The brutes!

YEZHOV: That's how low this vicious Fascist agent, this degenerate communist, has sunk to, God knows what else! These swine must be strangled! We cannot deal with them calmly ...

A VOICE: That scum! [Noise, more indignation in the room] What about Bukharin?

YEZHOV: I will now talk about Bukharin and Rykov. [Commotion in the room] ...

STALIN: We need to talk about them. They denied that they had any political platform. They had a platform, but it was awkward for them to show it. They concealed it. But there was a platform. What did it call for? For the restoration of private enterprise in industry, for the opening of our gates to foreign capital, especially to English capital.

BERIA: There's a scoundrel for you!

LIUBCHENKO: What swine.

Abu Bakr al-Baghdadi, 'Declare the Caliphate', 29 June 2014

Here is one of the most extraordinary speeches of the twenty-first century. During the summer of 2014, a new political and military force of jihadist militants that called itself the Islamic State took advantage of the chaos and war in Syria and Iraq to seize territory for itself. At its climax, IS armies captured the city of Mosul in Iraq and threatened the capital Baghdad. Little was known about this entity except it was a fanatical Sunni Muslim terror organisation that had grown out of al-Qaeda. But its nature was new: instead of remaining a mysterious terrorist cell, it aimed to found a new state and a society that channelled seventh-century puritanism and used twenty-first-century technology, filming and promoting its savagery on the internet through well-shot videos of beheadings and other atrocities. Its leader was a shadowy figure nicknamed 'The Ghost' who had taken the name of the first caliph Abu Bakr as his *nom de guerre*, but he was born in Iraq in 1971, studied Islam and then after the American invasion of Iraq led a terrorist group until he was arrested in February 2004. His time in prison allowed him to meet other jihadists and loyalists of the fallen dictator Saddam Hussein whom he would harness together. On his release he led al-Qaeda in Iraq and renamed it Islamic State. At its apogee he suddenly appears in this filmed sermon at the Great Mosque of Mosul to declare a Caliphate. But the brutalities of IS temporarily united an alliance of West and East that by 2019 had destroyed the so-called Caliphate. As for the caliph himself, his fate is unknown.

God has granted victory and conquest to your brothers and Mujahidin fighters after years of patience and holy struggle and enabled them to achieve their objective. So they have rushed to declare the Caliphate and appoint an Imam [sacred leader], a Caliph in charge which is a duty for all Muslims. It is a duty that has been lost for centuries which has been absent from reality, making many Muslims ignorant of it. I have been afflicted by this great affair, I have been afflicted by this trust, this heavy trust. I was appointed in charge of you though I am not the best of you nor am I better than you. So if you see me doing right, then help me and if you see me doing wrong, advise me and put me right.

Genghis Khan, 'The greatest pleasure', 13th century

The simple and brutal ambition of the conqueror of the world's greatest empire – and perhaps the most merciless definition of power ever stated by a potentate. Born around 1162 as Temujin of minor royalty in Mongolia, he adopted the title Genghis Khan – Lord of the World – and united the nomadic tribes of Mongolia to conquer most of Eurasia, from much of modern Russia and Central Asia to China, using killing and terror to overwhelm his enemies. After his death, Genghis Khan's successors divided the world into separate khanates. His chilling philosophy of conquest and domination is recounted in several histories including that of Rashid al-Din who was a son and grandson of courtiers of Hulugu Khan, Genghis' grandson and ruler of Persia. He would have heard this story. Genghis likes to ask his generals and family, 'What is the greatest joy and pleasure for a man?' One by one they choose the joys of hunting at which the world-emperor would reply, 'You didn't answer well,' defining happiness like this:

The greatest pleasure and joy for a man is to crush a rebel and to defeat an enemy, destroy him and take everything he possesses, seize his married women and make them weep, ride his fine and beautiful horses, and to fornicate with his beautiful wives and daughters and possess them completely.

Osama bin Laden, 'America is struck', 7 October 2001

A celebration of the 9/11 attack on America that killed over 2,000 innocent people. Bin Laden, born in Saudi Arabia, the son of a construction billionaire, was first roused to righteous fury by the Soviet invasion of Afghanistan in 1979 which seemed to encapsulate the struggle between a decadent secularity and sacred Islam. When he joined the mujahidin in Pakistan, he was backed by the CIA running President Reagan's policy to undermine the Soviets by deploying Islamic jihadis against them. It was a fatal mistake since bin Laden built on his training, prestige and contacts by founding al-Qaeda, 'the Base', a new jihadist terror organisation, backed by Saudi money and Saudi Salafists, to confront the West.

When the Iraqi invasion of Kuwait provoked the huge American military presence in Arabia, bin Laden mobilised for war against America, shifting his base first to Sudan in 1991 and then to Afghanistan in 1996, now under the control of the fundamentalist Taliban movement. From there he planned a spectacular new strike against America using hijacked airliners as colossal flying bombs. His attack on 11 September 2001 worked in that it provoked American wars against Afghanistan and then Iraq that were self-inflicted wounds. Bin Laden became the most wanted man in the world and teased America with recorded speeches but after his near capture in a battle at the Tora Bora caves in December 2001, he vanished for a decade, hiding at a house in Pakistan until he was discovered and executed in a raid by US Navy SEALs. By that time, the concept of jihad had been diverted to the Islamic State vision of a territorial caliphate. In the end, recordings of bin Laden showed that he did admit to the 9/11 terrorist attack but this early speech celebrates the atrocity without fully acknowledging his guilt.

Here is America struck by God Almighty in one of its vital organs, so that its greatest buildings are destroyed. Grace and gratitude to God. America has been filled with horror from north to south and east to west, and thanks be to God. What America is tasting now is only a copy of what we have tasted.

Our Islamic nation has been tasting the same for more than eighty years of humiliation and disgrace, its sons killed and their blood spilled, its sanctities desecrated.

God has blessed a group of vanguard Muslims, the forefront of Islam, to destroy America . . .

A million innocent children are dying at this time as we speak, killed in Iraq without any guilt. We hear no denunciation, we hear no edict from the hereditary rulers. In these days, Israeli tanks rampage across Palestine, in Ramallah, Rafah and Beit Jala and many other parts of the land of Islam, and we do not hear anyone raising his voice or reacting. But when the sword fell upon America after eighty years, hypocrisy raised its head up high bemoaning those killers who toyed with the blood, honour and sanctities of Muslims . . .

I say that the matter is very clear. Every Muslim, after this event, after the senior officials in the United States of America starting with the head of international infidels. Bush and his staff who went on a display of vanity with their men and horses, those who turned even the countries that believe in Islam against us – the group that resorted to God, the Almighty, the group that refuses to be subdued in its religion . . .

But when a few more than ten were killed in Nairobi and Dar es Salaam, Afghanistan and Iraq were bombed and hypocrisy stood behind the head of international infidels: the modern world's symbol of paganism, America, and its allies.

I tell them that these events have divided the world into two camps, the camp of the faithful and the camp of infidels. May God shield us and you from them.

Every Muslim must rise to defend his religion. The wind of faith is blowing and the wind of change is blowing to remove evil from the

Peninsula of Mohammed, peace be upon him.

As to America, I say to it and its people a few words: I swear to God that America will not live in peace before peace reigns in Palestine, and before all the army of infidels depart the land of Mohammed, peace be upon him.

God is the greatest and glory be to Islam.

Maximilien Robespierre, 'Virtue and terror', 5 February 1794

The visionary of modern terror. Robespierre was an ascetic lawyer from the small French town of Arras who became the advocate and organiser of the mass killings of the French Revolution. Coming to Paris as a member of the Estates-General and then the Constituent Assembly, he led the more radical Jacobin faction, supposedly coining the slogan *'Liberté, égalité, fraternité'* and arguing fervently for the execution of King Louis XVI. As opposition to the revolution intensified inside France and outside from Austria and Prussia, Robespierre pushed for a regime of what he called Virtue and Terror.

On 27 July 1793 Robespierre was chosen as a member of the twelve-man Committee of Public Safety, created by his ally Georges Danton. In April 1794, he turned on Danton, who was arrested and executed. Robespierre ruled France for a few terrible months. On 26 July 1794, he was so openly attacked in the Convention that he could not speak. As his critics suggested, it was Robespierre's betrayal of Danton, just weeks earlier, that struck him dumb. 'The blood of Danton chokes him!' cried a deputy, at which Robespierre answered: 'Is it Danton you regret? . . . Cowards! Why didn't you defend him?' After the debate, Robespierre was arrested but somehow escaped and was planning a coup when he and his conspirators were surrounded by government militia. He tried to shoot himself in the head but only managed to shatter his jaw. The executioner ripped off the bandage around his jaw at which he emitted a high-pitched scream of agony before the blade fell. At his apogee, he delivers this beautifully written hymn to killing that would provide the inspiration for much of the horror of the Bolshevik and Fascist Terrors of the twentieth century.

Citizen-representatives of the people. Some time ago we set forth the principles of our foreign policy; today we come to expound the principles of our internal policy. After having proceeded haphazardly for a long time, swept along by the movement of opposing factions, the representatives of the French people have finally demonstrated a character and a government. A sudden change in the nation's fortune announced to Europe the regeneration that had been effected in the national representation. But, to found and consolidate democracy, to achieve the peaceable reign of the constitutional laws, we must end the war of liberty against tyranny and pass safely across the storms of the revolution: such is the aim of the revolutionary system that you have enacted. Your conduct, then, ought also to be regulated by the stormy circumstances in which the republic is placed; and the plan of your administration must result from the spirit of the revolutionary government combined with the general principles of democracy.

Now, what is the fundamental principle of the democratic or popular government – that is, the essential spring which makes it move? It is virtue; I am speaking of the public virtue which effected so many prodigies in Greece and Rome and which ought to produce much more surprising ones in republican France; of that virtue which is nothing other than the love of country and of its laws.

But as the essence of the republic or of democracy is equality, it follows that the love of country necessarily includes the love of equality . . .

Not only is virtue the soul of democracy; it can exist only in that government . . .

Republican virtue can be considered in relation to the people and in relation to the government; it is necessary in both. When only the government lacks virtue, there remains a resource in the people's virtue; but when the people itself is corrupted, liberty is already lost.

Fortunately virtue is natural to the people, notwithstanding aristocratic prejudices. A nation is truly corrupted when, having by degrees lost its character and its liberty, it passes from democracy to aristocracy or to monarchy; that is the decrepitude and death of the body politic . . .

But when, by prodigious efforts of courage and reason, a people breaks the chains of despotism to make them into trophies of liberty; when by the force of its moral temperament it comes, as it were, out of the arms of the death, to recapture all the vigour of youth; when by turns it is sensitive and proud, intrepid and docile, and can be stopped neither by impregnable ramparts nor by the innumerable armies of the tyrants armed against it, but stops of itself upon confronting the law's image; then if it does not climb rapidly to the summit of its destinies, this can only be the fault of those who govern it.

. . . From all this let us deduce a great truth: the characteristic of popular government is confidence in the people and severity towards itself.

The whole development of our theory would end here if you had only to pilot the vessel of the Republic through calm waters; but the tempest roars, and the revolution imposes on you another task.

. . . We must smother the internal and external enemies of the Republic or perish with it; now in this situation, the first maxim of your policy ought to be to lead the people by reason and the people's enemies by terror.

If the spring of popular government in time of peace is virtue, the springs of popular government in revolution are at once virtue and terror: virtue, without which terror is fatal; terror, without which virtue is powerless. Terror is nothing other than justice, prompt, severe, inflex- ible; it is therefore an emanation of virtue; it is not so much a special principle as it is a consequence of the general principle of democracy applied to our country's most urgent needs.

It has been said that terror is the principle of despotic government. Does your government therefore resemble despotism? Yes, as the sword that gleams in the hands of the heroes of liberty resembles that with which the henchmen of tyranny are armed. Let the despot govern by terror his brutalised subjects; he is right, as a despot. Subdue by terror the enemies of liberty, and you will be right, as founders of the Republic. The government of the revolution is liberty's despotism against tyranny. Is force made only to protect crime? And is the thunderbolt not destined to strike the heads of the proud?

Nature has imposed upon every being the law of self-preservation. Crime massacres innocence to reign and innocence struggles with all its force in the hands of crime. Let tyranny but reign one day and the on the morrow there would not remain a single patriot. Until when will the fury of tyranny continue to be called justice and the justice of the people barbarity and rebellion? How tender they are to oppressors – how inexorable to the oppressed! Nevertheless it is necessary that one or the other should succumb. Indulgence for the royalists! exclaim certain men. Mercy for the wretches! No! Mercy for the innocent, mercy for the weak, mercy for the unfortunate, mercy for humanity!

Trials

Socrates, 'The unexamined life is not worth living', 399 BC

One of the greatest courtroom speeches that celebrates life before death. In 399 BC, Socrates faced trial in his native Athens for impiety and corrupting youth. Socrates, son of a stonemason and sculptor, was born in Athens, a democratic city-state that dominated a naval and trading empire. At the height of its power, Athens clashed with Sparta, the chief land power in Greece, leading to the thirty-year Peloponnesian War (431–404 BC) during which Socrates served, like his fellow citizens, as a hoplite infantryman, winning respect for his courage, and in one battle saving the Athenian commander Alcibiades from death. But Athens was defeated, and democracy was replaced by a murderous oligarchy imposed by Sparta. When the oligarchs were overthrown, democracy was restored – but the city must have been tense and vigilant after such catastrophe, a mood that would not tolerate a philosopher and teller of truths like Socrates.

This remarkable speech may have been written later by Socrates' philosophical heir, Plato, but it surely reflects the public speech he gives at his trial. In this amazing and jaunty address, he expresses his belief that wisdom, derived from self-knowledge, is the result of fearless self-examination and the confrontation of contradictions and lies; virtue is knowledge and engenders happiness; and no evil happens to a good man. Sentenced to death by drinking hemlock, Socrates refuses to escape into exile. Being Socrates, he describes the effect of his hemlock poisoning as it climbs his body, even discussing a sacrifice he had remembered before he died: 'Crito, we owe a cock to Asclepius. Please, don't forget to pay the debt.' Was he being ironical or just practical? Either way, he believed all philosophy is training for death.

There are many reasons why I am not grieved, O men of Athens, at the vote of condemnation. I expected it, and am only surprised that the votes are so nearly equal; for I had thought that the majority against me would have been far larger; but now, had thirty votes gone over to the other side, I should have been acquitted . . .

And so he [the judge] proposes death as the penalty. And what shall I propose on my part, O men of Athens? Clearly that which is my due. And what is my due? What return shall be made to the man who has never had the wit to be idle during his whole life; but has been careless of what the many care for – wealth, and family interests, and military offices, and speaking in the assembly, and magistracies, and plots, and parties. Reflecting that I was really too honest a man to be a politician and live, I did not go where I could do no good to you or to myself; but where I could do the greatest good privately to every one of you, thither I went, and sought to persuade every man among you that he must look to himself, and seek virtue and wisdom before he looks to his private interests, and look to the state before he looks to the interests of the state; and that this should be the order which he observes in all his actions. What shall be done to such a one? Doubtless some good thing, O men of Athens, if he has his reward; and the good should be of a kind suitable to him . . .

I speak rather because I am convinced that I never intentionally wronged anyone, although I cannot convince you – the time has been too short; if there were a law at Athens, as there is in other cities, that a capital cause should not be decided in one day, then I believe that I should have convinced you. But I cannot in a moment refute great slanders; and, as I am convinced that I never wronged another, I will assuredly not wrong myself. I will not say of myself that I deserve any evil, or propose any penalty. Why should I? Because I am afraid of the penalty of death which Meletus proposes? When I do not know whether death is a good or an evil, why should I propose a penalty which would certainly be an evil? Shall I say imprisonment? . . . Or shall the penalty be a fine, and imprisonment until the fine is paid? There is the same objection. I should have to lie in prison, for money I have none, and cannot pay. And if I say exile (and this may possibly be the penalty which you will affix), I must indeed be blinded by the love of life, if I am so irrational as to expect that when you, who are my own citizens, cannot endure my discourses and words, and have found them so grievous and odious that you will have no more of them, others are likely to endure me. No indeed, men of Athens, that is not very likely. And what a life should I lead, at my age, wandering from city to city, ever changing my place of exile, and always being driven out! For I am quite sure that wherever I go, there, as here, the young men will flock to me; and if I drive them away, their elders will drive me out at their request; and if I let them come, their fathers and friends will drive me out for their sakes.

Someone will say: Yes, Socrates, but cannot you hold your tongue, and then you may go into a foreign city, and no one will interfere with you? Now I have great difficulty in making you understand my answer to this. For if I tell you that to do as you say would be a disobedience to the God, and therefore that I cannot hold my tongue, you will not believe that I am serious; and if I say again that daily to discourse about virtue, and of those other things about which you hear me examining myself and others, is the greatest good of man, and that the unexamined life is not worth living, you are still less likely to believe me. Yet I say what is true, although a thing of which it is hard for me to persuade you . . .

Not much time will be gained, O Athenians, in return for the evil name which you will get from the detractors of the city, who will say that you killed Socrates, a wise man; for they will call me wise, even though I am not wise, when they want to reproach you. If you had waited a little while, your desire would have been fulfilled in the course of nature. For I am far advanced in years, as you may perceive, and not far from death. I am speaking now not to all of you, but only to those who have condemned me to death. And I have another thing to say to them: you think that I was convicted because I had no words of the sort which would have procured my acquittal – I mean, if I had thought fit to leave nothing undone or unsaid. Not so; the deficiency which led to my conviction was not of words – certainly not. But I had not the boldness or impudence or inclination to address you as you would have liked me to do, weeping and wailing and lamenting, and saying and doing many things which you have been accustomed to hear from others, and which, as I maintain, are unworthy of me. I thought at the time that I ought not to do anything common or mean when in danger: nor do I now repent of the style of my defence; I would rather die having spoken after my manner, than speak in your manner and live. For neither in war nor yet at law ought I or any man to use every way of escaping death. Often in battle there can be no doubt that if a man will throw away his arms, and fall on his knees before his pursuers, he may escape death; and in other dangers there are other ways of escaping death, if a man is willing to say and do anything.

The difficulty, my friends, is not to avoid death, but to avoid unrighteousness; for that runs faster than death. I am old and move slowly, and the slower runner has overtaken me, and my accusers are keen and quick, and the faster runner, who is unrighteousness, has overtaken them. And now I depart hence condemned by you to suffer the penalty of death – they too go their ways condemned by the truth to suffer the penalty of villainy and wrong; and I must abide by my award – let them abide by theirs. I suppose that these things may be regarded as fated, and I think that they are well.

And now, O men who have condemned me, I would fain prophesy to you; for I am about to die, and in the hour of death men are gifted with prophetic power. And I prophesy to you who are my murderers, that immediately after my departure punishment far heavier than you have inflicted on me will surely await you. Me you have killed because you wanted to escape the accuser, and not to give an account of your lives . . .

Let us reflect in another way, and we shall see that there is great reason to hope that death is a good; for one of two things – either death is a state of nothingness and utter unconsciousness, or, as men say, there is a change and migration of the soul from this world to another. Now if you suppose that there is no consciousness, but a sleep like the sleep of him who is undisturbed even by dreams, death will be an unspeakable gain . . . If death be of such a nature, I say that to die is gain; for eternity is then only a single night.

But if death is the journey to another place, and there, as men say, all the dead abide, what good, O my friends and judges, can be greater than this? If indeed when the pilgrim arrives in the world below, he is delivered from the professors of justice in this world, and finds the true judges who are said to give judgment there, Minos and Rhadamanthus and Aeacus and Triptolemus, and other sons of God who were righteous in their own life, that pilgrimage will be worth making. What would not a man give if he might converse with Orpheus and Musaeus and Hesiod and Homer? Nay, if this be true, let me die again and again . . .

Wherefore, O judges, be of good cheer about death, and know of a certainty, that no evil can happen to a good man, either in life or after death. He and his are not neglected by the gods; nor has my own approaching end happened by mere chance. But I see clearly that the time had arrived when it was better for me to die and be released from trouble; wherefore the oracle gave no sign. For which reason, also, I am not angry with my condemners, or with my accusers; they have done me no harm, although they did not mean to do me any good; and for this I may gently blame them.

Still I have a favour to ask of them. When my sons are grown up, I would ask you, O my friends, to punish them; and I would have you trouble them, as I have troubled you, if they seem to care about riches, or anything, more than about virtue; or if they pretend to be something when they are really nothing, then reprove them, as I have reproved you, for not caring about that for which they ought to care, and thinking that they are something when they are really nothing. And if you do this, both I and my sons will have received justice at your hands.

The hour of departure has arrived, and we go our ways – I to die, and you to live. Which is better God only knows.

Nikolai Yezhov, 'Shoot me quietly', 3 February 1940

Stalin's poison dwarf prepares to die. Yezhov was the diminutive Communist official and NKVD (secret police) boss who won Stalin's patronage by his brutal competence, fanatical paranoia and personal devotion to the witch hunt, arrest, torture and killing of around a million innocent victims, many of them Bolshevik leaders. But by 1938, Yezhov was daring to execute personal enemies and gathering evidence against Stalin himself and other leaders. He was falling apart under the pressure, drinking heavily, indulging in sexual escapades with men and women, and worrying about his declining favour with Stalin. Lavrenti Beria, a Georgian, was brought in as his deputy then successor and he was fired, then arrested and tried secretly. Knowing he is about to be executed, he reads this extraordinary confession to the court, intended to display his eternal devotion to Stalin and Party. Soon after this he was executed.

For a long time I have thought about what it will feel like to go to trial, how I should behave at the trial, and I have come to the conclusion that the only way I could hang on to life is by telling everything honestly and truthfully. Only yesterday, in a conversation with me, Beria said to me: 'Don't assume that you will necessarily be executed. If you will confess and tell everything honestly, your life will be spared.' After this conversation with Beria I decided: it is better to die, it is better to leave this earth as an honourable man and to tell nothing but the truth at the trial. At the preliminary investigation I said that I was not a spy, that I was not a terrorist, but they didn't believe me and beat me up horribly. During the twenty-five years of my party work I have fought honourably against enemies and have exterminated them. I have committed crimes for which I might well be executed. I will talk about them later. But I have not committed and am innocent of the crimes which have been imputed to me by the prosecution in its bill of indictment . . .

I did not organise any conspiracy against the party and the government. On the contrary, I used everything at my disposal to expose conspiracies ...

One may wonder why I would repeatedly place the question of the Cheka's sloppy work before Stalin if I was a part of an anti-Soviet conspiracy ...

Coming from the NKVD [People's Commissariat for Internal Affairs], I found myself at first alone. I didn't have an assistant. At first, I acquainted myself with the work, and only then did I begin my work by crushing the Polish spies who had infiltrated all departments of the organs of the Cheka. Soviet intelligence was in their hands. In this way, I, 'a Polish spy', began my work by crushing Polish spies. After crushing the Polish spies, I immediately set out to purge the group of turncoats. That's how I began my work for the NKVD. I personally exposed Molchanov and, along with him, also other enemies of the people, who had infiltrated the organs of the NKVD and who had occupied important positions in it. I had intended to arrest Liushkov, but he slipped out of my hands and fled abroad. I purged 14,000 chekists. But my great guilt lies in the fact that I purged so few of them. My practice was as follows: I would hand over the task of interrogating the person under arrest to one or another department head while thinking to myself: 'Go on, interrogate him today – tomorrow I will arrest you.' All around me there were enemies of the people, my enemies. I purged chekists everywhere. It was only in Moscow, Leningrad, and the Northern Caucasus that I did not purge them. I thought they were honest, but it turned out, in fact, that I had been harbouring under my wing saboteurs, wreckers, spies, and enemies of the people of other stripes ...

I have never taken part in an anti-Soviet conspiracy. If all the testimonies of the members of the conspiracy are carefully read, it will become apparent that they were slandering not only me but also the CC [Central Committee] and the government ...

I am charged with corruption as pertaining to my morals and private life. But where are the facts? I have been in the public eye of the party for twenty-five years. During these twenty-five years everyone saw me, everyone loved me for my modesty and honesty. I do not deny that I drank heavily, but I worked like a horse. Where is my corruption? I understand and honestly declare that the only cause for sparing my life would be for me to admit that I am guilty of the charges brought against me, to repent before the party and to implore it to spare my life. Perhaps the party will spare my life when taking my services into account. But the party has never had any need of lies, and I am once again declaring to you, that I was not a Polish spy, and I do not want to admit guilt to that charge because such an admission would only be a gift to Polish landowners, just as admitting guilt to espionage activity for England and Japan would only be a gift to English lords and Japanese samurai. I refuse to give such gifts to those gentlemen . . .

I'll now finish my final address. I ask the military collegium to grant me the following requests:

1. My fate is obvious. My life, naturally, will not be spared since I myself have contributed to this at my preliminary investigation. I ask only one thing: shoot me quietly, without putting me through any agony.
2. Neither the court nor the CC will believe in my innocence. If my mother is alive, I ask that she be provided for in her old age, and that my daughter be taken care of.
3. I ask that my relatives not be subjected to punitive measures because they are not guilty of anything.
4. I ask that the court investigate thoroughly the case of Zhurbenko, whom I considered and still consider to be an honest man devoted to the Leninist-Stalinist cause.
5. I request that Stalin be informed that I have never in my political life deceived the party, a fact known to thousands of persons who know my honesty and modesty.

I request that Stalin be informed that I am a victim of circumstances and nothing more, yet here enemies I have overlooked may have also had a hand in this. Tell Stalin that I shall die with his name on my lips.

Follies

Richard Nixon, 'No whitewash at the White House', 30 April 1973

The need to assert truthfulness is often a clear sign that mendacity is on the rampage. In politics, such insistence, often with simultaneous accusations that everyone else is lying, usually proves the case. And so it is with this speech. President Richard Nixon was a subtle and gifted statesman, particularly shrewd in matters of foreign policy, but he was even more tormented, devious, paranoid and obsessional than the average politician. During the 1972 presidential campaign, Nixon ordered a break-in at the offices of the Democratic Party's National Committee, at Washington's Watergate building. As reporters at the *Washington Post* investigated, aided by an FBI informant known as 'Deep Throat', Nixon and his henchmen tried desperately to cover up the original crime. Criminal prosecutions commenced against some presidential aides. Now as the evidence emerged that Nixon's top aides were involved, he is forced to sack them and promise to ensure that justice would be done while insisting on his own innocence. But he was involved. Investigators got access to tape recordings of the Oval Office where Nixon had ordered his aides to undermine the FBI investigation of the burglary. This was the so-called 'smoking gun' that destroyed his presidency. The repeated 'whiteness' in 'whitewash' and 'White House' became the very definition of lies and corruption. Faced with almost certain impeachment, Nixon was forced to resign.

Good evening.

I want to talk to you tonight from my heart on a subject of deep concern to every American.

In recent months, members of my Administration and officials of the Committee for the Re-Election of the President – including some of my closest friends and most trusted aides – have been charged with involvement in what has come to be known as the Watergate affair.

These include charges of illegal activity during and preceding the 1972 presidential election and charges that responsible officials participated in efforts to cover up that illegal activity.

The inevitable result of these charges has been to raise serious questions about the integrity of the White House itself. Tonight I wish to address those questions.

Last June 17, while I was in Florida trying to get a few days rest after my visit to Moscow, I first learned from news reports of the Watergate break-in. I was appalled at this senseless, illegal action, and I was shocked to learn that employees of the Re-Election Committee were apparently among those guilty.

I immediately ordered an investigation by appropriate government authorities. On September 15, as you will recall, indictments were brought against seven defendants in the case.

As the investigations went forward, I repeatedly asked those conducting the investigation whether there was any reason to believe that members of my Administration were in any way involved. I received repeated assurances that there were not. Because of these continuing reassurances, because I believed the reports I was getting, because I had faith in the persons from whom I was getting them, I discounted the stories in the press that appeared to implicate members of my Administration or other officials of the campaign committee.

Until March of this year, I remained convinced that the denials were true and that the charges of involvement by members of the White House Staff were false. The comments I made during this period, and the comments made by my press secretary on my behalf, were based on the information provided to us at the time we made those comments. However, new information then came to me which persuaded me that there was a real possibility that some of these charges were true, and suggesting further that there had been an effort to conceal the facts both from the public, from you, and from me.

As a result, on March 21, I personally assumed the responsibility for coordinating intensive new inquiries into the matter, and I personally ordered those conducting the investigations to get all the facts and to report them directly to me, right here in this office . . .

I was determined that we should get to the bottom of the matter, and that the truth should be fully brought out – no matter who was involved . . .

Today, in one of the most difficult decisions of my presidency, I accepted the resignations of two of my closest associates in the White House – Bob Haldeman [chief of staff], John Ehrlichman [domestic adviser] – two of the finest public servants it has been my privilege to know . . .

In any organization, the man at the top must bear the responsibility. That responsibility, therefore, belongs here, in this office. I accept it . . .

When I think of this office – of what it means – I think of all the things that I want to accomplish for this nation, of all the things I want to accomplish for you . . . We must maintain the integrity of the White House, and that integrity must be real, not transparent. There can be no whitewash at the White House.

Neville Chamberlain, 'Peace for our time', 30 September 1938

The speech that made the Second World War inevitable. Neville Chamberlain, British prime minister, was deceived and manipulated by Adolf Hitler at the Munich Conference. When Hitler, who had already swallowed Austria, demanded the right to annex the Sudetenland region of Czechoslovakia to protect its German majority, Chamberlain rushed back and forth between London and Germany, negotiating a peaceful way to give Hitler what he wanted. Assisted by the French premier Daladier and by Hitler's ally, the Fascist dictator of Italy, Mussolini, Chamberlain believed, despite all the obvious signals of Hitler's own promises and rhetoric over the past decade, that this would satisfy the German Führer. The charismatic, theatrical and manipulative Hitler ran rings around the plodding umbrella-wielding Englishman. On Chamberlain's return from Munich, having shamefully betrayed the Czechs by forcing them to hand over a large section of their country to Hitler, he delivers this triumphant speech. Hitler broke his promises by then annexing the rump of Czechoslovakia. By then even Chamberlain realised his mistake and guaranteed Polish borders. Hitler, still believing he could intimidate the feckless democracies personified by this Englishman and his umbrella, invaded Poland. It was war. The words 'peace for our time' remain shorthand for naivety, delusion and folly.

My good friends, for the second time in our history a British prime minister has returned from Germany bringing peace with honour. I believe it is peace for our time. Go home and get a nice quiet sleep.

Adolf Hitler, 'I am at the head of the strongest army in the world', 11 December 1941

The speech that lost Hitler the war. In June 1941, Hitler attacked Soviet Russia. Then in December, Japan attacked America at Pearl Harbor. There was no need for Hitler to declare war against America too. And yet, in an astonishing and suicidal act of arrogance and hubris, he does just that, ensuring that Britain, America and Russia, the three greatest powers on earth, would unite to destroy him. This speech justifies Hitler's attack on Russia – at this moment his troops are being pushed back in brutal fighting outside Moscow – and his declaration of war against America. For a view inside Hitler's mind, its vision of Germanic racial supremacy and vicious antisemitism is worth the read . . .

Deputies, Men of the German Reichstag!

. . . After the renewed refusal of my peace offer in January 1940 by the then British Prime Minister and the clique which supported or else dominated him, it became clear that this war – against all reasons of common sense and necessity – must be fought to its end. You know me, my old Party companions: you know I have always been an enemy of half measures or weak decisions. If Providence has so willed that the German people cannot be spared this fight, then I can only be grateful that it entrusted me with the leadership in this historic struggle which, for the next 500 or 1,000 years, will be described as decisive, not only for the history of Germany, but for the whole of Europe and indeed the whole world . . .

With every month I became more convinced that the plans of the men in the Kremlin aimed at the domination and annihilation of all Europe. I have had to submit to the nation the full extent of the Russian military preparations. At a time when Germany had only a few divisions in the provinces bordering on Russia it would have been evident to a blind man that a concentration of power of singular and world historic dimensions was taking place, and this was not in order to defend something which was threatened, but merely in order to attack an object it did not seem possible to defend. The lightning conclusion of the Western campaign, however, robbed the Moscow overlords of their hope of an early flagging of German power. This did not alter their intentions – it merely led to a postponement of the date on which they intended to strike. In the summer of 1941 they thought the time was ripe. A new Mongol invasion was now to sweep Europe . . .

The Urals do not form the frontier of our Continent, but the eternal line which divides the Eastern and Western conceptions of life. There was a time when Europe was that Greek island into which Nordic tribes had penetrated in order to light a torch for the first time which from then onwards began slowly but surely to brighten the world of man. When these Greeks repulsed the invasion of the Persian conquerors they not only defended their homeland, which was Greece, but that idea which we call Europe today. And then Europe travelled from Hellas to Rome. With the Greek spirit and Greek culture, the Roman way of thinking and Roman statesmanship were combined. An Empire was created which, to this day, has not been equalled in its significance and creative power, let alone outdone. When, however, the Roman legions were defending Rome against the African onslaught of Carthage and at last gained a victory, again it was not Rome they were fighting for, but the Europe of that time, which consisted of the Graeco-Roman world.

The next incursion against this homestead of European culture was carried out from the distant East. A terrible stream of barbarous, uncultured hordes sallied forth from the interior of Asia deep into the heart of the European Continent, burning, looting, murdering – a true scourge of the Lord. In the battle of the Catalaunian fields the West was formed. On the ruins of Rome the West was built, and its defence was a task not only of the Romans, but also above all of the Teutons [Germanic peoples]. In centuries to come the West, enlightened by Greek culture, built the Roman Empire and then expanded by the colonization of the Teutons was able to call itself Europe. Whether it was the German Emperor who was repelling the attacks from the East on the Field of Lech or whether Africa was being pushed back from Spain in long fighting, it was also a struggle of a developing Europe against a profoundly alien outside world. Once Rome had been given its due for the creative defence of this continent, Teutons took over the defence . . .

Thus it was not England who brought culture to the Continent, but the Anglo-Saxon and Norman branches of the Germanic nation that moved from our continent to the British Island and made possible her development, which is certainly unique in history. In just the same way, it was not America who discovered Europe, but the other way around. And everything which America has not drawn from Europe may well appear worthy of admiration to a Juda-ised mixed race; Europe, on the other hand, sees in it a sign of cultural decay . . .

But the chief role was played by Soviet Russia . . .

In view of the mortal danger from Soviet Russia, not only to the German Reich but to all Europe, I decided, if possible, to give the signal myself to attack a few days before the outbreak of this conflict.

Today, we have overwhelming and authentic proof that Russia intended to attack; we are also quite clear about the date on which the attack was to take place. In view of the great danger, the extent of which we are only now fully aware, I can only thank God that He enlightened me at the proper time and that He gave me the strength to do what had to be done! Millions of German soldiers may thank Him for their lives, and all of Europe for its very existence.

This much I may state today: had this wave of over 20,000 tanks, hundreds of divisions, tens of thousands of guns, accompanied by more than 10,000 aircraft, suddenly moved against the Reich, Europe would have been lost. Fate has destined a number of nations to forestall this attack, to ward it off with the sacrifice of their blood . . .

Had the German Reich not faced the enemy with her soldiers and arms, a flood would have swept over Europe, which once and for all would have finished the ridiculous British idea of maintaining the

European balance of power in all its senselessness and stupid tradition.

[...]

Roosevelt's New Deal legislation was all wrong: it was actually the biggest failure ever experienced by one man ...

He was strengthened in this resolve by the Jews around him. Their Old Testament thirst for revenge thought to see in the United States an instrument for preparing a second 'Purim' for the European nations which were becoming increasingly antisemitic. The full diabolical meanness of Jewry rallied round this man, and he stretched out his hands to them.

Thus began the increasing efforts of the American President to create conflicts, to do everything to prevent conflicts from being peacefully solved. For years this man harboured one desire – that a conflict should break out somewhere in the world ...

We have seen what the Jews have done in Soviet Russia. We have made the acquaintance of the Jewish Paradise on earth. Millions of German soldiers have been able to see this country where the international Jews have destroyed people and property. The President of the United States ought finally to understand – I say this only because of his limited intellect – that we know that the aim of this struggle is to destroy one State after another. But the present German Reich has nothing more in common with the old Germany. And we, for our part, will now do what this provocateur has been trying so hard to do for years. Not only because we are the ally of Japan, but also because Germany and Italy have enough insight and strength to comprehend that, in these historic times, the existence or non-existence of the nations is being determined, perhaps for all time. We clearly see what the rest of the world intends for us. They reduced democratic Germany to starvation, and they seek to exterminate the National Socialist Germany of today.

[...]

In the whole history of the German nation, of nearly 2,000 years, it has never been so united as today and, thanks to National Socialism it will remain united in the future ...

As a consequence of the further extension of President Roosevelt's policy, which is aimed at unrestricted world domination and dictatorship, the United States together with England have not hesitated from using any means to deny the rights of the German, Italian and Japanese nations the prerequisites for their vital natural existence. The governments of the United States and of England have therefore resisted every reasonable effort to bring about a better New Order in the world, not only now but also for all time . . .

The Three Powers have therefore concluded the following Agreement, which was signed in Berlin today:

'In their unshakable determination not to lay down arms until the joint war against the United States and England reaches a successful conclusion, the German, Italian, and Japanese governments have agreed on the following:

'Germany, Italy and Japan will wage the common war forced upon them by the United States and England with all the means of power at their disposal, to a victorious conclusion . . .'

Ever since my last peace proposal of July 1940 was rejected, we have realized that this struggle has to be fought out to its last implications. We National Socialists are not surprised that the Anglo-Saxon-Jewish-Capitalist World finds itself now in a united front with Bolshevism: we have always found them in the same company. We have concluded the struggle successfully inside Germany and have destroyed our adversaries after 14 years of struggle for power. When, 23 years ago, I decided to enter political life and to lift this nation out of its decline, I was a nameless, unknown soldier. Many among you know how difficult were the first few years of this struggle. From the time when the movement consisted of seven men, until we took over power in January 1933, the path was so miraculous that only Providence itself with its blessing could have made this possible.

Today I am at the head of the strongest army in the world, the most gigantic air force and a proud navy. Behind and around me stands the Party with which I became great and which has become great through me. The enemies I see before me are the same enemies as 20 years ago, but the path before us cannot be compared with the road we have already taken . . .

At a time when thousands of our best men have given their lives, anyone in the homeland who betrays the sacrifices made at the Front must expect to forfeit his life. Regardless of the pretext with which an attempt is made to disrupt this German Front, to undermine the will to resist of our people, to weaken the authority of the regime, to sabotage the achievements of the Home Front, he shall die for it! But the difference is that the soldier at the Front who makes will be held in the highest honour, whereas he who debases that sacrifice dies in dishonour and disgrace.

Our enemies must not deceive themselves. In the 2,000 years of recorded German history, our people have never been more determined and united than today. The Lord of the Universe has treated us so well in recent years that we bow in gratitude to a Providence which has allowed us to be members of such a great nation. We thank Him that our deeds of honour may also be recorded in the eternal book of German history!

Power

Theodora, 'Imperial purple is the noblest burial sheet', AD 532

The speech that saved an emperor. Justinian I was assisted in all things by his formidable wife, Theodora. She was the daughter of the bear-keeper of one of the chariot-racing factions of Constantinople – and she probably was a courtesan until she met Emperor Justin's nephew Justinian who succeeded him on the throne. Her sexual exploits, recounted by Procopius, are lubricious and athletic but clearly exaggerated. Early in his reign, Justinian faced a revolution in the burning streets of Constantinople. As they panic and prepare to flee for their lives, Theodora stiffens their resolve in this, the very definition of fearless ambition in the face of mortal danger – better to be killed and buried in a shroud of royal purple than die obscurely in exile. Justinian stays, slaughters 30,000 of his enemies and rebuilds the city, going on to reconquer Italy and North Africa.

My lords, the present occasion is too serious to allow me to follow the convention that a woman should not speak in a man's council. Those whose interests are threatened by extreme danger should think only of the wisest course of action, not of conventions.

In my opinion, flight is not the right course, even if it should bring us to safety. It is impossible for a person, having been born into this world, not to die; but for one who has reigned it is intolerable to be a fugitive. May I never be deprived of this purple robe, and may I never see the day when those who meet me do not call me empress.

If you wish to save yourself, my lord, there is no difficulty. We are rich; over there is the sea, and yonder are the ships. Yet reflect for a moment whether, when you have once escaped to a place of security, you would not gladly exchange such safety for death. As for me, I agree with the adage that the imperial purple is the noblest burial sheet.

Josef Stalin, 'We need new blood', 16 October 1952

The last terrifying speech of an ageing tyrant. Stalin, in his seventies, had ruled Russia for thirty years, killing tens of millions as he wiped out recalcitrant peasants and potential enemies. He had won the Second World War against Hitler, taking Berlin and conquering an empire in Eastern Europe. Although unchallenged in his total supremacy, he believed that bloodletting was the best tool for managing his empire, while his own morose paranoia intensified with his age and declining health.

At this Plenum of the Central Committee, he surprises everyone by suddenly giving this impromptu speech. Here we can hear the real voice of Stalin, informal and sinister. When he suggests promoting new young leaders over his old henchmen and hints that he himself is getting older and soon must retire, everyone knows they must insist – desperately – that he remain Leader. When he attacks his veteran lieutenants Molotov and Mikoyan, who are sitting miserably in the room, everyone realises they have been chosen to be denounced and then exe-cuted. When he mentions Molotov's wife, Zhemchuzhina, they knew that she may already have been shot for the sins of indis-cretion, being Jewish and being best friends with Stalin's late wife Nadya who committed suicide in 1932. As Stalin attacks Molotov for backing Jewish aspirations, the rabidly antisemitic dictator is laying out the accusation that his old comrade is an American-Zionist agent. (Here is the leftist antisemitism that has resurfaced in the twenty-first century.) Stalin chose to attack these comrades because they were the last two left alive who knew and worked with Lenin: Molotov was his most likely successor. The room listens to his speech with horror – and his devoted henchman Malenkov rushes to the podium, waving his hands frantically to encourage shouts of devotion, to demand that Stalin remain Leader. A new Terror is beginning. The arrests start.

But it was too late: Stalin suffered a cerebral haemorrhage and on 5 March 1953, he died. This speech remained secret until the 1990s.

STALIN: Yes, we did hold the Congress of our party. It went very well, and many of you might think that full harmony and unity exists among us. But we have not this harmony and unity of thought. Some of you are even opposed and do not like our decision.

They say, why do we need an enlarged Central Committee [CC]? But isn't it self-evident that we need new blood and new strength? ... We are getting older and shall sooner or later die, but we must think into whose hands we shall give this torch of our great undertaking, who will carry it onward and reach the goal of communism. For this we need younger people with more energy, dedicated comrades and political leaders ...

Is it not self-evident that we must lift up the importance and the role of our party and its party committees? Can we afford not to follow the desire of Lenin to improve the work of the party constantly? All this needs a flow of younger blood into the leadership ... We must, as Communists, be self-critical and also critical of others.

There has been criticism of comrades Molotov and Mikoyan by the Central Committee.

Comrade Molotov – the most dedicated to our cause. He shall give his life for the cause of the party. But we cannot overlook his weakness in certain aspects of his work. Comrade Molotov as our Minister of Foreign Affairs, finding himself at a 'slippery' diplomatic reception, gave assurance to a British diplomat that the capitalists can start to publish bourgeois newspapers in our country. Why? Was that the place to give such an assurance, without the knowledge of the CC CPSU [Communist Party of the Soviet Union]? Is it not self-evident that the bourgeoisie is our class enemy and to promote bourgeois newspapers among our party people, besides doing harm, shall not bring us any benefit? If this were allowed to transpire, we could foresee circumstances where the attacks against Socialism and the CPSU would be started, first very subtly then overtly. This is the first political mistake of comrade V. M. Molotov.

What about the incorrect suggestion by Molotov to give the Crimea to Soviet Jews? This is a flagrant mistake of comrade Molotov. Why was this even proposed? On what grounds did comrade Molotov make this proposal? We have a Jewish Autonomous Republic. What else is still needed? There are many other minority nations that have now their own Autonomous Regions and also Autonomous Republics . . . is this not enough now? Or is this meant not to trust the Constitution of the USSR and its policy on nationalities? Comrade Molotov is not appointed by anyone to be a lawyer for pursuing the territorial pretensions of the Union of Soviet Socialist Republics! This is the second mistake of our esteemed comrade V. M. Molotov! Thus, in this respect comrade Molotov is not correct in his proclamations as a member of the Politburo. The CC CPSU has categorically defeated his suggestion.

Comrade Molotov has such deep respect for his wife, that no sooner have the CC or the Politburo made numerous decisions on this or that question, that this decision immediately is conveyed to Molotov's wife Zhemchuzhina and all of her friends. Her friends, as is well known to all of you here, are not to be trusted, as former situations have shown. It is of course not the way that a member of the CPSU CC Politburo should behave.

Now regarding comrade Mikoyan. He is categorically against, and thus he agitates against, any taxes for the Soviet peasants. What is it that is not clear to our esteemed comrade A. I. Mikoyan?

FARMER DEPUTY: . . . We do not agree with the suggestion put forward by comrade Mikoyan. [Mikoyan comes to the speaker's tribune and starts to defend his policies]

STALIN: Well comrade Mikoyan, you are lost in your own policies and you are now trying to get the members of the CC to be lost with you. Are you still unclear? [Molotov comes to the speaker's tribune and completely admits his mistakes before the CC, but states that he 'is and will always be a faithful disciple of Stalin']

STALIN: [interrupting Molotov] This is nonsense. I have no students at all. We are all students of the great Lenin. [Stalin suggests that they continue the agenda point by point and elect a new ruling Politburo, renamed a Presidium] . . . With no Politburo, there is now elected a Presidium of the CC CPSU in the enlarged CC and in the Secretariat of the CC CPSU, altogether 36 members . . .

A VOICE: We need to elect comrade Stalin as the General Secretary of the CC and Chairman of the Council of Ministers of the USSR.

STALIN: No! I am asking that you relieve me of the two posts!

MALENKOV: Comrades! We should all unanimously ask comrade Stalin, our leader and our teacher, to be again the General Secretary of the CC CPSU.

Abraham Lincoln, 'Government of the people, by the people, for the people', 19 November 1863

The power of this masterpiece lies partly in its location, on the fresh battlefield of Gettysburg, where over 50,000 men have recently been killed and buried in the most terrible battle of the American Civil War, partly in its timing, at the height of the fighting when other battles are raging across America, and partly in its brevity, but above all in Lincoln's celebrated mastery of language, economy of expression and brilliance as a phrasemaker.

Four score and seven years ago our fathers brought forth on this continent a new nation, conceived in liberty and dedicated to the proposition that all men are created equal. Now we are engaged in a great civil war, testing whether that nation or any nation so conceived and so dedicated can long endure. We are met on a great battlefield of that war. We have come to dedicate a portion of that field as a final resting place for those who here gave their lives that that nation might live. It is altogether fitting and proper that we should do this. But in a larger sense, we cannot dedicate, we cannot consecrate, we cannot hallow this ground. The brave men, living and dead who struggled here have consecrated it far above our poor power to add or detract. The world will little note nor long remember what we say here, but it can never forget what they did here. It is for us the living rather to be dedicated here to the unfinished work which they who fought here have thus far so nobly advanced. It is rather for us to be here dedicated to the great task remaining before us – that from these honoured dead we take increased devotion to that cause for which they gave the last full measure of devotion – that we here highly resolve that these dead shall not have died in vain, that this nation under God shall have a new birth of freedom, and that government of the people, by the people, for the people shall not perish from the earth.

Donald Trump, 'Make America great again', 16 June 2015

The launch of an unlikely presidential campaign that changed the world. A real-estate developer and television reality host rides the golden elevator in his gaudy flagship building – Trump Tower, New York City – to declare he is running for the American presidency. He is not a conventional candidate but he turns out to be an astute communicator who could orate for many hours in a discursive, bombastic, brazen style that expresses the passion, nationalism and anger of his base of voters. Here is the rambling speech that starts it all. It's worth reading in full – his entire presidency is right here.

Wow. Whoa. That is some group of people. Thousands.

So nice, thank you very much. That's really nice. Thank you. It's great to be at Trump Tower. It's great to be in a wonderful city, New York. And it's an honor to have everybody here. This is beyond anybody's expectations. There's been no crowd like this.

And, I can tell, some of the candidates, they went in. They didn't know the air-conditioner didn't work. They sweated like dogs.

They didn't know the room was too big, because they didn't have anybody there. How are they going to beat ISIS? I don't think it's gonna happen.

Our country is in serious trouble. We don't have victories anymore. We used to have victories, but we don't have them. When was the last time anybody saw us beating, let's say, China in a trade deal? They kill us. I beat China all the time. All the time.

When did we beat Japan at anything? They send their cars over by the millions, and what do we do? When was the last time you saw a Chevrolet in Tokyo? It doesn't exist, folks. They beat us all the time.

When do we beat Mexico at the border? They're laughing at us, at our stupidity. And now they are beating us economically. They are not our friend, believe me. But they're killing us economically.

The US has become a dumping ground for everybody else's problems.

Thank you. It's true, and these are the best and the finest. When Mexico sends its people, they're not sending their best. They're not sending you. They're not sending you. They're sending people that have lots of problems, and they're bringing those problems with us. They're bringing drugs. They're bringing crime. They're rapists. And some, I assume, are good people.

But I speak to border guards and they tell us what we're getting. And it only makes common sense. It only makes common sense. They're sending us not the right people.

It's coming from more than Mexico. It's coming from all over South and Latin America, and it's coming probably – probably – from the Middle East. But we don't know. Because we have no protection and we have no competence, we don't know what's happening. And it's got to stop and it's got to stop fast.

Islamic terrorism is eating up large portions of the Middle East. They've become rich. I'm in competition with them.

They just built a hotel in Syria. Can you believe this? They built a hotel. When I have to build a hotel, I pay interest. They don't have to pay interest, because they took the oil that, when we left Iraq, I said we should've taken.

So now ISIS has the oil, and what they don't have, Iran has. And in 19 – and I will tell you this, and I said it very strongly, years ago, I said – and I love the military, and I want to have the strongest military that we've ever had, and we need it more now than ever. But I said, 'Don't hit Iraq,' because you're going to totally destabilize the Middle East. Iran is going to take over the Middle East, Iran and somebody else will get the oil, and it turned out that Iran is now taking over Iraq. Think of it. Iran is taking over Iraq, and they're taking it over big league.

We spent $2 trillion in Iraq, $2 trillion. We lost thousands of lives, thousands in Iraq. We have wounded soldiers, who I love, I love – they're great – all over the place, thousands and thousands of wounded soldiers. And we have nothing. We can't even go there. We have nothing. And every time we give Iraq equipment, the first time a bullet goes off in the air, they leave it.

Last week, I read 2,300 Humvees – these are big vehicles – were left behind for the enemy. 2,000? You would say maybe two, maybe four? 2,300 sophisticated vehicles, they ran, and the enemy took them.

Last quarter, it was just announced our gross domestic product – a sign of strength, right? But not for us. It was below zero. Whoever heard of this? It's never below zero . . .

A lot of people up there can't get jobs. They can't get jobs, because there are no jobs, because China has our jobs and Mexico has our jobs. They all have jobs . . .

Our enemies are getting stronger and stronger by the way, and we as a country are getting weaker. Even our nuclear arsenal doesn't work.

It came out recently they have equipment that is thirty years old. They don't know if it worked. And I thought it was horrible when it was broadcast on television, because boy, does that send signals to Putin and all of the other people that look at us and they say, 'That is a group of people, and that is a nation that truly has no clue. They don't know what they're doing. They don't know what they're doing.'

We have a disaster called the big lie: Obamacare. Obamacare . . .

I've watched the politicians. I've dealt with them all my life. If you can't make a good deal with a politician, then there's something wrong with you. You're certainly not very good. And that's what we have representing us. They will never make America great again. They don't even have a chance. They're controlled fully – they're controlled fully by the lobbyists, by the donors, and by the special interests, fully.

Yes, they control them. Hey, I have lobbyists. I have to tell you. I have lobbyists that can produce anything for me. They're great. But you know what? It won't happen. It won't happen. Because we have to stop doing things for some people, but for this country, it's destroying our country. We have to stop, and it has to stop now.

Now, our country needs – our country needs a truly great leader, and we need a truly great leader now. We need a leader that wrote The Art of the Deal.

We need a leader that can bring back our jobs, can bring back our manufacturing, can bring back our military, can take care of our vet[eran]s. Our vets have been abandoned.

And we also need a cheerleader.

You know, when President Obama was elected, I said, 'Well, the one thing I think he'll do well. I think he'll be a great cheerleader for the country. I think he'd be a great spirit.'

He was vibrant. He was young. I really thought that he would be a great cheerleader.

He's not a leader. That's true. You're right about that.

But he wasn't a cheerleader. He's actually a negative force. He's been a negative force. He wasn't a cheerleader; he was the opposite.

We need somebody that can take the brand of the United States and make it great again. It's not great again.

We need – we need somebody – we need somebody that literally will take this country and make it great again. We can do that.

And, I will tell you, I love my life. I have a wonderful family. They're saying, 'Dad, you're going to do something that's going to be so tough.'

You know, all of my life, I've heard that a truly successful person, a really, really successful person and even modestly successful cannot run for public office. Just can't happen. And yet that's the kind of mindset that you need to make this country great again.

So ladies and gentlemen . . . I am officially running . . . for president of the United States, and we are going to make our country great again . . .

But they all said, a lot of the pundits on television, 'Well, Donald will never run, and one of the main reasons is he's private and he's probably not as successful as everybody thinks.'

So I said to myself, you know, nobody's ever going to know unless I run, because I'm really proud of my success. I really am . . . And I have assets – big accounting firm, one of the most highly respected – 9 billion 240 million dollars.

And I have liabilities of about $500 million. That's long-term debt, very low interest rates.

In fact, one of the big banks came to me and said, 'Donald, you don't have enough borrowings. Could we loan you $4 billion?' I said, 'I don't need it. I don't want it. And I've been there. I don't want it.'

But in two seconds, they give me whatever I wanted. So I have a total net worth, and now with the increase, it'll be well over $10 billion. But here, a total net worth of – net worth, not assets, not – a net worth, after all debt, after all expenses, the greatest assets – Trump Tower, 1290 Avenue of the Americas, Bank of America building in San Francisco, 40 Wall Street, sometimes referred to as the Trump building right opposite the New York – many other places all over the world.

So the total is $8,737,540,000 . . . I'm not doing that to brag, because you know what? I don't have to brag. I don't have to, believe it or not.

I'm doing that to say that that's the kind of thinking our country needs. We need that thinking. We have the opposite thinking.

We have losers. We have losers. We have people that don't have it. We have people that are morally corrupt. We have people that are selling this country down the drain . . .

I would build a great wall, and nobody builds walls better than me, believe me, and I'll build them very inexpensively, I will build a great, great wall on our southern border. And I will have Mexico pay for that wall.

Mark my words.

Nobody would be tougher on ISIS than Donald Trump. Nobody.

I will find – within our military, I will find the General Patton or I will find General MacArthur, I will find the right guy. I will find the guy that's going to take that military and make it really work. Nobody, nobody will be pushing us around.

I will stop Iran from getting nuclear weapons. And we won't be using a man like Secretary Kerry that has absolutely no concept of negotiation, who's making a horrible and laughable deal, who's just being tapped along as they make weapons right now, and then goes into a bicycle race at 72 years old, and falls and breaks his leg. I won't be doing that. And I promise I will never be in a bicycle race. That I can tell you.

I will immediately terminate President Obama's illegal executive order on immigration, immediately . . .

Sadly, the American dream is dead.

But if I get elected president I will bring it back bigger and better and stronger than ever before, and we will make America great again.

Thank you. Thank you very much.

Aung San Suu Kyi, 'It is not power that corrupts, but fear', July 1991

Aung San Suu Kyi was born to a tradition of power, the youngest daughter of one of the founding fathers of independent Burma, now known as Myanmar. Aung San, the Communist and nationalist nicknamed 'The Major General', had served as a minister for the Japanese and British, and was assassinated in 1947. When the vast country of Burma, with its many ethnic minorities, was granted independence it became a parliamentary democracy but, in 1962, as the minorities pushed for a more federal state, General Ne Win seized power, brutally enforcing an isolated socialistic dictatorship.

Marrying an Englishman and spending much of her time in British exile, Aung returned to Burma to look after her mother just as students and other protestors staged a spontaneous uprising in 1998. The military crushed the uprising – and several that followed. Aung San Suu Kyi, who had become the symbol of free Burma and peaceful protest, rallied her followers as a National League of Democracy but, surviving an assassination attempt, she was put under house arrest. Her party won a majority of seats in subsequent elections despite government pressure but she was not allowed to stand. She was awarded the Sakharov Prize (which honours those who have defended human rights and freedom of thought) but was unable to collect it. Here is the speech she was not allowed to give. In 2015, in the first free elections since 1990, her party again won a huge majority and while a nominee of the generals became president she was appointed State Counsellor, a role similar to prime minister. But in security and financial matters, the generals did as they wished, crushing ethnic groups and sponsoring the persecution of the Muslim Rohingya minority, which exposes the realities of the compromise Aung had made.

It is not power that corrupts, but fear.

Fear of losing power corrupts those who wield it and fear of
the scourge of power corrupts those who are subject to it. Most
Burmese are familiar with the four *a-gati*, the four kinds of corruption.
Chanda-gati, corruption induced by desire, is deviation from the right
path in pursuit of bribes or for the sake of those one loves. *Dosa-gati* is
taking the wrong path to spite those against whom one bears ill will,
and *moga-gati* is aberration due to ignorance. But perhaps the worst
of the four is *bhaya-gati*, for not only does *bhaya*, fear, stifle and slowly
destroy all sense of right and wrong, it so often lies at the root of the
other three kinds of corruption. Just as *chanda-gati*, when not the result
of sheer avarice, can be caused by fear of want or fear of losing the
goodwill of those one loves, so fear of being surpassed, humiliated or
injured in some way can provide the impetus for ill will.

And it would be difficult to dispel ignorance unless there is freedom
to pursue the truth unfettered by fear. With so close a relationship
between fear and corruption it is little wonder that in any society where
fear is rife, corruption in all forms becomes deeply entrenched . . .

Emerald cool we may be. As water in cupped hands. But oh that we
might be. As splinters of glass. In cupped hands.

Glass splinters, the smallest with its sharp, glinting power to defend
itself against hands that try to crush, could be seen as a vivid symbol of
the spark of courage that is an essential attribute of those who would
free themselves from the grip of oppression . . .

The quintessential revolution is that of the spirit, born of an intellectual conviction of the need for change in those mental attitudes and
values which shape the course of a nation's development. A revolution
which aims merely at changing official policies and institutions with
a view to an improvement in material conditions has little chance of
genuine success. Without a revolution of the spirit, the forces which
produced the iniquities of the old order would continue to be operative,
posing a constant threat to the process of reform and regeneration.

. . . Saints, it has been said, are the sinners who go on trying. So free
men are the oppressed who go on trying and who in the process make

themselves fit to bear the responsibilities and to uphold the disciplines which will maintain a free society. Among the basic freedoms to which men aspire that their lives might be full and uncramped, freedom from fear stands out as both a means and an end. A people who would build a nation in which strong, democratic institutions are firmly established as a guarantee against state-induced power must first learn to liberate their own minds from apathy and fear . . .

Xi Jinping, 'History is our best teacher', 14 May 2017

The speech that may change the world. Since the 1990s it has been obvious to everyone that China is the rising world power. For millennia, under a succession of dynasties from Qin through Tang and Yuan up to the seventeenth-century Manchus, China was the dominant civilisation of the East, linked by trade, culture and war through Central Asia – the so-called Silk Road – to the Middle East and Europe. But in the nineteenth century, China declined radically, preyed upon by predatory European powers. In 1911, the monarchy fell and the empire disintegrated while Japan swallowed wads of territory. In 1949, the Chinese Communists, led by the charismatic and merciless Mao Zedong, seized control, and launched a series of radical convulsions culminating in the Cultural Revolution. Only after Mao's death in 1976 did his successor, the pragmatic Deng Xiaoping, introduce the duality of total Communist control (he ordered the massacre of protestors in Tiananmen Square in 1987) and free economic prosperity. Deng initiated an economic boom of astonishing proportions with China's GDP rising from $263 billion when his reforms started in 1979 to a colossal $14 trillion in 2018, making it the second biggest economy in the world after America. In 2012, Xi Jinping, son of a vice-premier who had been sent to work in the provinces during the Cultural Revolution, became president and swiftly achieved the authority of the Core Leader, a power not seen since Mao, with the ability to rule for life. While imposing stricter political control at home, he launched his Belt and Road initiative to promote Chinese world power and link China to the Middle East, Africa and the rest of the world, building ports, supply chains, sea routes and railways, one of the most ambitious geostrategic visions ever pursued. Ports are being built, loans are being offered, political influence purchased and won by the new superpower that will inevitably clash with America.

Ladies and Gentlemen, Dear Friends,

In this lovely season of early summer when every living thing is full of energy, I wish to welcome all of you, distinguished guests representing over 100 countries, to attend this important forum on the Belt and Road Initiative held in Beijing. This is indeed a gathering of great minds. In the coming two days, I hope that by engaging in full exchanges of views, we will contribute to pursuing the Belt and Road Initiative, a project of the century, so that it will benefit people across the world.

Over 2,000 years ago, our ancestors, trekking across vast steppes and deserts, opened the transcontinental passage connecting Asia, Europe and Africa, known today as the Silk Road. Our ancestors, navigating rough seas, created sea routes linking the East with the West, namely, the maritime Silk Road . . .

Spanning thousands of miles and years, the ancient silk routes embody the spirit of peace and cooperation, openness and inclusiveness, mutual learning and mutual benefit. The Silk Road spirit has become a great heritage of human civilization . . .

History is our best teacher. The glory of the ancient silk routes shows that geographical distance is not insurmountable. If we take the first courageous step towards each other, we can embark on a path leading to friendship, shared development, peace, harmony and a better future . . .

In the autumn of 2013, respectively in Kazakhstan and Indonesia, I proposed the building of the Silk Road Economic Belt and the Twenty-first Century Maritime Silk Road, which I call the Belt and Road Initiative. As a Chinese saying goes, 'Peaches and plums do not speak, but they are so attractive that a path is formed below the trees.'

As we often say in China, 'The beginning is the most difficult part.' A solid first step has been taken in pursuing the Belt and Road Initiative. We should build on the sound momentum generated to steer the Belt and Road Initiative toward greater success. In pursuing this endeavour, we should be guided by the following principles:

First, we should build the Belt and Road into a road for peace. The ancient silk routes thrived in times of peace, but lost vigour in times of war. The pursuit of the Belt and Road Initiative requires a peaceful and stable environment . . . Second, we should build the Belt and Road into a road of prosperity . . . Third, we should build the Belt and Road into a road of opening up . . . Fourth, we should build the Belt and Road into a road of innovation . . . Fifth, we should build the Belt and Road into a road connecting different civilizations. An ancient Chinese saying goes, 'A long journey can be covered only by taking one step at a time.' Similarly, there is an Arab proverb which says that the Pyramid was built by piling one stone on another. In Europe, there is also the saying that 'Rome wasn't built in a day'. The Belt and Road Initiative is a great undertaking which requires dedicated efforts. Let us pursue this initiative step by step and deliver outcomes one by one. By doing so, we will bring true benefit to both the world and all our people!

Peacemakers

Anwar al-Sadat, 'I have come to Jerusalem, as the City of Peace', 20 November 1977

It is a dangerous act of courage to make peace in the Middle East. In November 1977, the Egyptian leader flew to Israel and dramatically offered peace in this famous speech to Israel's Knesset (parliament). Sadat was one of the military officers, along with Gamal Abdul Nasser, who formed the secret Free Officers that in 1952 overthrew King Farouk and expelled his British backers. Sadat became Nasser's vice-president in 1964. But when Nasser, diminished by the total defeat by Israel in the Six Day War and by heart disease, died in 1970, Sadat succeeded, determined to wage war to reduce Israeli dominance. On Yom Kippur 1973, Sadat, with his Syrian ally, launched a surprise attack on Israel that briefly threatened Israeli survival and shattered Israeli overconfidence. This success allowed Sadat to seek a peace with the newly elected Israeli prime minister Menachem Begin that would restore Sinai to Egypt. But it cost Sadat his life. In 1981 he was assassinated at a military parade by members of the Muslim Brotherhood. Yet Egypt is still at peace with Israel.

Peace and the mercy of God Almighty be upon you and may peace be for us all, God willing . . .

I come to you today on solid ground, to shape new life, to establish peace. We all, on this land, the land of God; we all, Muslims, Christians and Jews, worship God and no one but God. God's teachings and commandments are love, sincerity, purity and peace.

I do not blame all those who received my decision – when I announced it to the entire world before the Egyptian People's Assembly – with surprise and amazement. Some, gripped by the violent surprise, believed that my decision was no more than verbal juggling to cater for world public opinion. Others, still, interpreted it as political tactics to camouflage my intention of launching a new war. I would go as far as to tell you that one of my aides at the presidential office contacted me at a late hour following my return home from the People's Assembly and sounded worried as he asked me: 'Mr President, what would be our reaction if Israel should actually extend an invitation to you?' I replied calmly, 'I will accept it immediately' . . .

Any life lost in war is a human life, irrespective of its being that of an Israeli or an Arab. A wife who becomes a widow is a human being entitled to a happy family life, whether she be an Arab or an Israeli. Innocent children who are deprived of the care and compassion of their parents are ours, be they living on Arab or Israeli land.

. . . Let us be frank with each other as we answer this important question: How can we achieve permanent peace based on justice?

. . . The first fact: no one can build his happiness at the expense of the misery of others.

The second fact: never have I spoken or will ever speak in two languages. Never have I adopted or will adopt two policies. I never deal with anyone except in one language, one policy, and with one face.

The third fact: direct confrontation and a straight line are the nearest and most successful methods to reach a clear objective.

The fourth fact: the call for permanent and just peace, based on respect for the UN resolutions, has now become the call of the whole world.

. . . The fifth fact: and this is probably the clearest and most prominent, is that the Arab nation, in its drive for permanent peace based on justice, does not proceed from a position of weakness or hesitation, but it has the potential of power and stability which tells of a sincere will for peace.

. . . I would also wish to warn you in all sincerity; I warn you against some thoughts that could cross your minds; frankness makes it incumbent upon me to tell you the following:

First: I have not come here for a separate agreement between Egypt and Israel. This is not part of the policy of Egypt.

. . . Second: I have not come to you to seek a partial peace, namely to terminate the state of belligerency at this stage, and put off the entire problem to a subsequent stage . . . I have come to you so that together we might build a durable peace based on justice, to avoid the shedding of one single drop of blood from an Arab or an Israeli.

. . . Here, I would go back to the answer to the big question: how can we achieve a durable peace based on justice? In my opinion . . . the answer is neither difficult nor impossible, despite long years of feud, blood vengeance, spite and hatred, and breeding generations on concepts of total rift and deep-rooted animosity.

. . . You want to live with us in this part of the world. In all sincerity, I tell you, we welcome you among us, with full security and safety. This, in itself, is a tremendous turning point; one of the landmarks of a decisive historical change. We used to reject you. We had our reasons and our claims, yes.

We used to brand you as 'so-called' Israel, yes . . . Yet, today I tell you, and declare it to the whole world, that we accept to live with you in permanent peace based on justice. We do not want to encircle you or be encircled ourselves by destructive missiles ready for launching, nor by the shells of grudges and hatred. I have announced on more than one occasion that Israel has become a *fait accompli*, recognized by the world, and that the two super powers have undertaken the responsibility of its security and the defence of its existence.

As we really and truly seek peace, we really and truly welcome you to live among us in peace and security.

. . . I have come to Jerusalem, as the City of Peace, which will always remain as a living embodiment of coexistence among believers of the three religions. It is inadmissible that anyone should conceive the special status of the City of Jerusalem within the framework of annexation or expansionism, but it should be a free and open city for all believers.

. . . Complete withdrawal from the Arab territories occupied in 1967 is a logical and undisputed fact. Nobody should plead for that. Any talk about permanent peace based on justice, and any move to ensure our coexistence in peace and security in this part of the world, would become meaningless, while you occupy Arab territories by force of arms.

. . . As for the Palestinians' cause, nobody could deny that it is the crux of the entire problem. The cause of the Palestinian people and their legitimate rights are no longer ignored or denied today by anybody. Rather, nobody who has the ability of judgement can deny or ignore it . . . I hail the Israeli voices that called for the recognition of the Palestinian people's rights to achieve and safeguard peace. Here I tell you, ladies and gentlemen, that it is no use refraining from recognizing the Palestinian people and their rights to statehood and rights of return. We, the Arabs, have faced this experience before, with you and with the reality of Israeli existence. The struggle took us from war to war, from victims to more victims, until you and we have today reached the edge of a horrifying abyss and a terrifying disaster, unless, together, we seize the opportunity, today, of a durable peace based on justice . . .

Yitzhak Rabin, 'Enough of blood and tears', 13 September 1993

In September 1993, the Israeli Prime Minister Yitzhak Rabin and the Chairman of the Palestine Liberation Organization Yasser Arafat met at the White House under the aegis of President Bill Clinton to sign a peace treaty to end the conflict between the two peoples that had raged since the creation of Israel in 1948. At the time there was great hope and excitement. The PLO recognized Israel which recognized the PLO as the representative of the Palestinians and in turn established a Palestinian Authority which, when the final terms on all matters such as Jerusalem and the status of refugees were agreed, could become a state. Both men had led harsh lives of war. Arafat had organized terror attacks on civilians while Rabin had been the chief of staff who commanded the Israeli victories in the Six Day War. Now as prime minister, his speech, appropriate for this laconic and shy man, is a study in simplicity and honesty. The treaty cost Rabin his life. While attending a peace rally on 4 November 1995, he was assassinated by a Jewish fanatic.

Mr President, Ladies and Gentlemen,

This signing of the Israeli-Palestinian Declaration of Principles, here today, is not so easy either for myself, as a soldier in Israel's wars, or for the people of Israel, nor to the Jewish people in the Diaspora who are watching us now with great hope, mixed with apprehension. It is certainly not easy for the families of the victims of the wars, violence, terror, whose pain will never heal. For the many thousands who have defended our lives in their own, and even sacrificed their lives for our own for them, this ceremony has come too late. Today, on the eve of an opportunity for peace and perhaps an end of violence and wars we remember each and every one of them with everlasting love.

We have come from Jerusalem, the ancient and eternal capital of the

Jewish people. We have come from an anguished and grieving land. We have come from a people, a home, a family, that has not known a single year, not a single month, in which mothers have not wept for their sons. We have come to try and put an end to the hostilities, so that our children, our children's children, will no longer experience the painful cost of war, violence and terror. We have come to secure their lives and to ease the sorrow and the painful memories of the past, to hope and pray for peace.

Let me say to you, the Palestinians: We are destined to live together on the same soil, in the same land. We, the soldiers who have returned from battle stained with blood, we who have seen our relatives and friends killed before our eyes, we who have attended their funerals and cannot look into the eyes of their parents, we who have come from a land where parents bury their children, we who have fought against you, the Palestinians –

We say to you today in a loud and a clear voice: enough of blood and tears. Enough. We have no desire for revenge. We harbour no hatred towards you. We, like you, are people who want to build a home, to plant a tree, to love, to live side by side with you in dignity, in empathy, as human beings, as free men. We are today giving peace a chance, and saying again to you: Enough. Let us pray that a day will come when we all will say: Farewell to arms.

We wish to open a new chapter in the sad book of our lives together, a chapter of mutual recognition, of good neighbourliness, of mutual respect, of understanding. We hope to embark on a new era in the history of the Middle East. Today, here in Washington, at the White House, we will begin a new reckoning in relations between peoples, between parents tired of war, between children who will not know war . . .

Our inner strength, our high moral values, have been derived for thousands of years from the Book of Books, in one of which, Koheleth, we read:

To every thing there is a season, and a time to every purpose under heaven:

A time to be born, and a time to die;
A time to kill, and a time to heal;
A time to weep and a time to laugh;
A time to love, and a time to hate;
A time of war, and a time of peace.

Ladies and Gentlemen, the time for peace has come.

. . . In the Jewish tradition, it is customary to conclude our prayers with the word 'Amen'. With your permission, men of peace, I shall conclude with words taken from the prayer recited by Jews daily, and whoever of you volunteer, I would ask the entire audience to join me in saying 'Amen':

'He maketh peace in His high places. He shall make peace for us and for all of Israel. And they shall say: Amen.'

Revolution

Georges Danton, 'Dare, dare again, always dare!', 2 September 1792

The best speaker of the French Revolution who was consumed by the very forces he unleashed. Born in 1759 in the provinces of France, strapping and athletic, coarse and passionate, Georges Danton rose to power as a revolutionary radical. His speeches were said to 'shake the domes of the halls'. Danton encouraged the September Massacres of 1792, voted for the abolition of the monarchy and then the beheading of King Louis XVI. When France was threatened with invasion, he famously responded, 'The kings of Europe would dare challenge us? We throw them the head of a king!' Elected to the Committee of Public Safety alongside his comrade Robespierre, whom he regarded as a mediocrity, he helped organise the Terror. But then, accused of financial misconduct by his enemies including Robespierre, he was tried and guillotined. Here, faced with the advancing armies of the *ancien régime*, he displays all his oratorical power in the greatest speech of the Revolution.

It is gratifying to the ministers of a free people to have to announce to them that their country will be saved. All are stirred, all are excited, all burn to fight. You know that Verdun is not yet in the power of our enemies. You know that its garrison swears to immolate the first who breathes a proposition of surrender.

One portion of our people will proceed to the frontiers, another will throw up intrenchments, and the third with pikes will defend the hearts of our cities. Paris will second these great efforts. The commissioners of the Commune will solemnly proclaim to the citizens the invitation to arm and march to the defence of the country. At such a moment you can proclaim that the capital deserves well of all France.

At such a moment this National Assembly becomes a veritable committee of war. We ask that you concur with us in directing this sublime movement of the people, by naming commissioners who will second us in these great measures. We ask that anyone refusing to give personal service or to furnish arms shall be punished with death. We ask that a set of instructions be drawn up for the citizens to direct their movements. We ask that couriers be sent to all the departments to notify them of the decrees that you proclaim here. The tocsin we are about to ring is not an alarm signal; it sounds the charge on the enemies of our country. To conquer them we must dare, dare again, always dare, and France is saved!

Mao Zedong, 'The Chinese people have stood up!', 21 September 1949

Communist victory in China changes the world. Chairman Mao, the ruthless revolutionary, radical Marxist-Stalinist and visionary ruler, was also a brilliant writer of speeches and articles, a master of phrases, an amateur poet and historical enthusiast as well as an outstanding military tactician who defined modern theories of guerrilla warfare. Born in Hunan in 1893, son of a well-off farmer, he helped found the Chinese Communist Party. In the early 1930s, he created the Red Army and came to dominate the Party as its chairman, leading its armies.

When the Japanese started their invasion of China, Mao negotiated a temporary alliance with the Kuomintang Nationalist leader Chiang Kai-shek. After the end of the Second World War, backed by huge military aid from Stalin, Mao conquered China as the Kuomintang fled to Taiwan. On 1 October 1949 in Tiananmen Square, Beijing, Mao declared the People's Republic of China. Liquidating the land-owning and educated classes in purges, killing millions, he created a new China. When the Americans intervened in the Korean War, he sent in the Red Army to turn the tide of the war and subsequently received nuclear weaponry from Russia. Mao launched the Great Leap Forward to make China an industrial power, leading to a famine in which tens of millions perished. When his own comrades challenged his programmes, he organised his Cultural Revolution to terrorise the Party and promote his total dictatorship through a near-religious cult. It culminated in mass killings and deportations, cultural sterility, economic and political chaos and, after a failed coup attempt, the flight and death of his chosen successor Lin Biao. In 1972, Mao challenged Soviet power by opening China to US President Nixon. He ruled until his death in 1976.

Fellow Delegates, the Political Consultative Conference so eagerly awaited by the whole nation is herewith inaugurated ...

It is because we have defeated the reactionary Kuomintang government backed by US imperialism that this great unity of the whole people has been achieved. In a little more than three years the heroic Chinese People's Liberation Army, an army such as the world has seldom seen, crushed all the offensives launched by the several million troops of the US-supported reactionary Kuomintang government and turned to the counter-offensive and the offensive ...

Fellow Delegates, we are all convinced that our work will go down in the history of mankind, demonstrating that the Chinese people, comprising one-quarter of humanity, have now stood up. The Chinese have always been a great, courageous and industrious nation; it is only in modern times that they have fallen behind. And that was due entirely to oppression and exploitation by foreign imperialism and domestic reactionary governments ... Ours will no longer be a nation subject to insult and humiliation. We have stood up. Our revolution has won the sympathy and acclaim of the people of all countries. We have friends all over the world ... As long as we persist in the people's democratic dictatorship and unite with our foreign friends, we shall always be victorious ...

Let the domestic and foreign reactionaries tremble before us! Let them say we are no good at this and no good at that. By our own indomitable efforts we the Chinese people will unswervingly reach our goal.

The heroes of the people who laid down their lives in the People's War of Liberation and the people's revolution shall live for ever in our memory!

Hail the victory of the People's War of Liberation and the people's revolution!

Hail the founding of the People's Republic of China! ...

Vladimir Ilyich Lenin, 'Power to the Soviets', September 1917

Here in his own words is the furious force and political genius of Lenin. In September 1917, the Provisional Government of Alexander Kerensky was decaying fast – and here Lenin, Marxist fanatic, founder of the Bolshevik faction, long-time exile from Russia, announces it is time to seize power. But the speech conceals its real meaning: when Lenin says 'all power to the Soviets', he actually means all power to his own tiny clique; when he says 'dictatorship of the proletariat', he means himself. Soon afterwards, the Bolsheviks seized power, creating the Soviet Union that, at the cost of millions of innocent lives, ruled Russia until 1991. Lenin's body is still revered in Moscow where it lies embalmed like a Communist saint in Red Square.

The key question of every revolution is undoubtedly the question of state power. Which class holds power decides everything . . .

The question of power cannot be evaded or brushed aside, because it is the key question determining everything in a revolution's development, and in its foreign and domestic policies. It is an undisputed fact that our revolution has 'wasted' six months in wavering over the system of power; it is a fact resulting from the wavering policy of the Socialist Revolutionaries and Mensheviks. In the long run, these parties' wavering policy was determined by the class position of the petty bourgeoisie, by their economic instability in the struggle between capital and labour.

The whole issue at present is whether the petty-bourgeois democrats have learned anything during these great, exceptionally eventful six months.

If not, then the revolution is lost, and only a victorious uprising of the proletariat can save it. If they have learned something, the establishment of a stable, unwavering power must be begun immediately.

Only if power is based, obviously and unconditionally, on a majority of the population can it be stable during a popular revolution, i.e., a revolution which rouses the people, the majority of the workers and peasants, to action. Up to now state power in Russia has virtually remained in the hands of the bourgeoisie, who are compelled to make only particular concessions (only to begin withdrawing them the following day), to hand out promises (only to fail to carry them out), to search for all sorts of excuses to cover their domination (only to fool the people by a show of 'honest coalition'), etc., etc. In words it claims to be a popular, democratic, revolutionary government, but in deeds it is an anti-popular, undemocratic, counter-revolutionary, bourgeois government. This is the contradiction which has existed so far and which has been a source of the complete instability and inconsistency of power, of that 'ministerial leapfrog' in which the SRs and Mensheviks have been engaged with such unfortunate (for the people) enthusiasm . . .

There is no middle course. This has been shown by experience. Either all power goes to the Soviets both centrally and locally, and all land is given to the peasants immediately, pending the Constituent Assembly's decision, or the landowners and capitalists obstruct every step, restore the landowners' power, drive the peasants into a rage and carry things to an exceedingly violent peasant revolt.

Only the dictatorship of the proletariat and the poor peasants is capable of smashing the resistance of the capitalists, of displaying truly supreme courage and determination in the exercise of power, and of securing the enthusiastic, selfless and truly heroic support of the masses both in the army and among the peasants.

Power to the Soviets – this is the only way to make further progress gradual, peaceful and smooth, keeping perfect pace with the political awareness and resolve of the majority of the people and with their own experience. Power to the Soviets means the complete transfer of the country's administration and economic control into the hands of the workers and peasants, to whom nobody would dare offer resistance and who, through practice, through their own experience, would soon learn how to distribute the land, products and grain properly.

Ruhollah Khomeini, 'I shall smash this government in the teeth', February 1979

How the Imam of the Iranian Revolution takes power. Ruhollah Khomeini, born in 1902, in Khomeyn, wrote poetry in his youth and studied the Koran and Iran's Twelver Shiism in the local capital Arak and then the Holy City of Qom. He spent much of his life opposing the modernising autocracy of the two Pahlavi shahs (kings).

When Shah Mohammed Reza Pahlavi assumed absolute power in the 1950s and launched his White Revolution which included the liberation and education of women, Khomeini denounced the shah as 'wretched and miserable'. After riots, Khomeini was arrested and forced into exile in Iraq then Paris. Spreading his rabidly anti-Pahlavi, anti-Western message through taped speeches on cassettes that were copied and secretly distributed around Iran, he became the leading voice of opposition. Khomeini expanded the theory of *velayat-el faqih*, the 'Guardianship of the Islamic Jurist', to propose a theocracy in Iran, rule by Islamic clerics – namely himself – while democracy was seen as a sort of Western prostitution. In 1979, vast protests led to the downfall of the shah and Khomeini's return from exile, who was not just an Ayatollah but now hailed as the sacred Imam. He took power as the Supreme Leader and executed members of the old regime but he created a hybrid political system with an elected presidency and parliament. All real power remained with the Supreme Leader who challenged 'America the Great Satan' in the hostage crisis of 1979–81 then fought neighbouring Iraq for ten brutal years. He died in 1989. Here is one of the speeches he gave on his arrival before a crowd so vast it may have been one of the largest in human history. As he puts it, 'I shall smash this government in the teeth . . .'

I must tell you that Mohammad Reza Pahlavi, that evil traitor, has gone. He fled and plundered everything. He destroyed our country and filled our cemeteries. He ruined our country's economy. Even the projects he carried out in the name of progress, pushed the country towards decadence. He suppressed our culture, annihilated people and destroyed all our manpower resources. We are saying this man, his government, his majlis are all illegal. If they were to continue to stay in power, we would treat them as criminals and would try them as criminals. I shall appoint my own government. I shall smash this government in the teeth. I shall determine the government with the backing of this nation, because this nation accepts me.

Warmongers

Urban II, 'Enter upon the road to the Holy Sepulchre', 27 November 1095

Christian Holy War! Here is the speech that launches the Crusades. Jerusalem, the Holy City, had been held by the Muslims since AD 638 during the period when Islamic Holy War, led by the Arab caliphs, had conquered an empire. Yet Christians throughout Europe constantly visited Jerusalem on pilgrimage and revered the city. Now the Muslims were fragmented into warring fiefdoms and Christian pilgrims were repeatedly slaughtered. Simultaneously, Christian Europe was shattered by warring barons, the Church regarded as corrupt. Hence in 1095, the dynamic and visionary Pope Urban II, keen to redirect the fighting spirit of Europe and reinvigorate and purify the Church, devised a Christian doctrine of Holy War. (Several versions of this speech were recorded, this one by Robert the Monk.) The result was a European fever of armed pilgrimage as different groups from all Christian countries – peasants, priests, knights, barons and dukes – crossed the continent and converged into different armies. Altogether as many as 80,000 people set off on the long journey to Jerusalem. Most perished but in 1099 a tiny army of around 12,000 stormed Jerusalem, killing everyone inside, Muslims and Jews, in a frenzied slaughter. Jerusalem became the capital of a Crusader kingdom until the city was recaptured by Saladin, on behalf of Islam, in 1187. But the crusading spirit endured for four centuries.

Oh, race of Franks, race from across the mountains, race chosen and beloved by God as shines forth in very many of your works, set apart from all nations by the situation of your country, as well as by your catholic faith and the honour of the holy church! To you our discourse is addressed and for you our exhortation is intended. We wish you to know what a grievous cause has led us to Your country, what peril threatening you and all the faithful has brought us.

From the confines of Jerusalem and the city of Constantinople a horrible tale has gone forth and very frequently has been brought to our ears, namely, that a race from the kingdom of the Persians, an accursed race, a race utterly alienated from God, a generation forsooth which has not directed its heart and has not entrusted its spirit to God, has invaded the lands of those Christians and has depopulated them by the sword, pillage and fire; it has led away a part of the captives into its own country, and a part it has destroyed by cruel tortures; it has either entirely destroyed the churches of God or appropriated them for the rites of its own religion. They destroy the altars, after having defiled them with their uncleanness. They circumcise the Christians, and the blood of the circumcision they either spread upon the altars or pour into the vases of the baptismal font.

When they wish to torture people by a base death, they perforate their navels, and dragging forth, the extremity of the intestines, bind it to a stake; then with flogging they lead the victim around until the viscera having gushed forth the victim falls prostrate upon the ground. Others they bind to a post and pierce with arrows. Others they compel to extend their necks and then, attacking them with naked swords, attempt to cut through the neck with a single blow. What shall I say of the abominable rape of the women? To speak of it is worse than to be silent . . . On whom therefore is the labour of avenging these wrongs and of recovering this territory incumbent, if not upon you? You, upon whom above other nations God has conferred remarkable glory in arms, great courage, bodily activity, and strength to humble the hairy scalp of those who resist you . . .

Let the Holy Sepulchre of the Lord our Saviour [Jerusalem], which is possessed by unclean nations, especially incite you, and the holy places which are now treated with ignominy and irreverently polluted with their filthiness. Oh, most valiant soldiers and descendants of invincible ancestors, be not degenerate, but recall the valour of your progenitors . . .

Let none of your possessions detain you, no solicitude for your family

affairs, since this land which you inhabit, shut in on all sides by the seas
and surrounded by the mountain peaks, is too narrow for your large
population; nor does it abound in wealth; and it furnishes scarcely food
enough for its cultivators. Hence it is that you murder one another, that
you wage war, and that frequently you perish by mutual wounds. Let
therefore hatred depart from among you, let your quarrels end, let wars
cease, and let all dissensions and controversies slumber. Enter upon the
road to the Holy Sepulchre; seize that land from the wicked race, and
subject it to yourselves. That land, which as the Scripture says 'floweth
with milk and honey', was given by God into the possession of the
children of Israel. Jerusalem is the navel of the world; the land is fruitful
above others, like another paradise of delights. This the Redeemer of the
human race has made illustrious by His advent, has beautified by resi-
dence, has consecrated by suffering, has redeemed by death, has glorified
by burial. This royal city, therefore, situated at the centre of the world, is
now held captive by His enemies, and is in subjection to those who do
not know God, to the worship of the heathens. She seeks therefore and
desires to be liberated, and does not cease to implore you to come to her
aid. From you especially she asks succour, because, as we have already
said, God has conferred upon you above all nations great glory in arms.
Accordingly undertake this journey for the remission of your sins, with the
assurance of the imperishable glory of the kingdom of heaven . . .

    Whoever, therefore, shall determine upon this holy pilgrimage and
shall make his vow to God to that effect and shall offer himself to Him
as a living sacrifice, holy, acceptable unto God, shall wear the sign of the
cross of the Lord on his forehead or on his breast. When, truly, having
fulfilled his vow he wishes to return, let him place the cross on his back
between his shoulders. Such, indeed, by the twofold action will fulfil the
precept of the Lord, as He commands in the Gospel, 'He that taketh not
his cross and followeth after me, is not worthy of me.'

Cato the Elder, 'Carthage must be destroyed!', 149 BC

The speech that condemns an entire civilisation to total destruction. Cato the Elder was a Roman politician, soldier and orator in the era of the rivalry between Rome and Carthage. Still an oligarchical republic ruled by two annually elected consuls and a senate, Rome had expanded outside its Italian base to become a Mediterranean power but its growth was challenged by another Mediterranean empire. Carthage was originally a Phoenician city state linked to Tyre in today's Lebanon, which developed a republican system of government with two annually elected magistrates and a council of elders. The city also appointed generals who gradually amassed greater power. The two empires clashed in Sardinia and Sicily leading to three Punic Wars. In the first, Carthage lost Sicily but a brilliant family of generals, led by Hamilcar Barca then his son Hannibal, created a new empire in Spain. In the second war (218–202 BC), Hannibal invaded Italy itself and nearly took Rome but was ultimately defeated. A punishing treaty defanged Carthage but when it started to recover, Cato the Elder started to relentlessly promote the idea that the city should be obliterated. Plutarch reports that from 153 BC to his death in 149 aged eighty-five, Cato ended every speech in the Senate 'on any subject whatsoever' with the same words: *Delenda est Carthago*. The repetition made its mark. In 149 BC Rome provoked a new war that led to the total destruction of Carthage; its population was sold into slavery, its buildings burned for seventeen days and what was left was ploughed over and sown with salt.

Who are the ones who have often violated the treaty? Who are the ones who have waged war most cruelly? . . . Who are the ones who have ravaged Italy? The Carthaginians. Who are the ones who demand forgiveness? The Carthaginians. See then how it would suit them. *Delenda est Carthago* – Carthage Must be Destroyed!

Genocide

Adolf Hilter, 'The annihilation of the Jewish race in Europe', 30 January 1939

How Hitler warned the world that he planned to exterminate the Jewish people.

By the start of 1939, Hitler had managed to obliterate any opposition within Germany by violence, propaganda and racism, demonising the Jews, but also using his own cult of personality and his extraordinary success at outmanoeuvring the Western democracies to consume Austria and carve up Czechoslovakia. As he prepares to swallow the remnant of Czechoslovakia and then destroy Poland, he believes that the unique providence of Germany's opportunity and his own personality, plus his belief that he himself would die young, mean he must now risk everything, even a world war, to achieve German imperial and racial conquest. On 30 January 1939, the sixth anniversary of Adolf Hitler's election as chancellor, he addresses the Reichstag with this sinister 'prophecy' that should the Western powers resist his conquests, the Jews of Europe will pay the price with their annihilation. Few took this explicit threat seriously, but Hitler was frankly warning of his own plan for the Holocaust while also following the antisemitic tradition of blaming the Jews for their own persecution. His overweening and hubristic vanity, almost a Christ-complex, is on display as he reflects, without irony, 'I have very often been a prophet.'

In the course of my life I have very often been a prophet, and have usually been ridiculed for it. During the time of my struggle for power it was in the first instance only the Jewish race that received my prophecies with laughter when I said that I would one day take over the leadership of the State, and with it that of the whole nation, and that I would then among other things settle the Jewish problem. Their laughter was uproarious, but I think that for some time now they have

been laughing on the other side of their face. Today I will once more be
a prophet: if the international Jewish financiers in and outside Europe
should succeed in plunging the nations once more into a world war,
then the result will not be the Bolshevizing of the earth, and thus the
victory of Jewry, but the annihilation of the Jewish race in Europe!

Heinrich Himmler, 'The Jewish people are going to be exterminated', 4 October 1943

This speech is more distressing, chilling and disgusting than Hitler's. It is such an unsettling read even now that it is not often found in anthologies like this. Four years after Hitler's warning in 1939, the elimination of the Jewish people is now reality. A diabolical crime on an industrial scale without parallel in human history is in progress in villages, towns and death camps across Europe.

Heinrich Himmler was the senior Nazi entrusted by Hitler with the murder of many millions of innocent men, women and children who happened to be Jewish, the result of fanatical antisemitism that blamed all the ills of the world on Jewish people. The slaughter began with the conquest of Poland and the subsequent invasion of Russia. Himmler, a Bavarian school-master's son who had failed as a chicken farmer and joined the Nazis as an early Hitler devotee, had built up the SS as the Führer's praetorian guard and ideological and racial vanguard for special tasks. At first he sent *Einsatzgruppen* murder squads to kill Jews in mass shootings, then favoured the use of gas to spare the 'humanity' of the executioners and increase the industrial capacity of the killing, leading to the building of co-lossal death camps where victims were gassed then incinerated. This speech – surely the most wicked thing in history – given in secret in Pozna to a select audience of SS officials – is made all the more horrifying by Himmler's claims that the SS child-killers were knights of a new age and by his plangent tone of self-pity and self-sacrifice. Six million Jews were killed before the Nazis were defeated. Astonishingly, few of the perpetrators were punished and Himmler himself evaded trial by committing suicide.

I also want to speak to you here, in complete frankness, of a really grave chapter. Amongst ourselves, for once, it shall be said quite openly, but all the same we will never speak about it in public. Just as we did not hesitate on 30 June 1934 [the Night of the Long Knives] to do our duty as we were ordered, and to stand comrades who had erred against the wall and shoot them, and we never spoke about it and we never will speak about it. It was a matter of natural tact that is alive in us, thank God, that we never talked about it amongst ourselves, that we never discussed it. Each of us shuddered and yet each of us knew clearly that the next time he would do it again if it were an order, and if it were necessary. I am referring here to the evacuation of the Jews, the extermination of the Jewish people. This is one of the things that is easily said: 'The Jewish people are going to be exterminated,' that's what every Party member says. 'Sure, it's in our programme, elimination of the Jews, extermination – it'll be done.' And then they all come along, the 80 million worthy Germans, and each one has his one decent Jew. Of course, the others are swine, but this one, he is a first-rate Jew. Of all those who talk like that, not one has seen it happen, not one has had to go through with it. Most of you men know what it is like to see a hundred corpses side by side, or five hundred or a thousand. To have stood fast through this – and except for cases of human weakness – to have stayed decent, that has made us hard. This is an unwritten and never-to-be-written page of glory in our history, for we know how difficult it would be for us if today – under bombing raids and the hardships and deprivations of war – if we were still to have the Jews in every city as secret saboteurs, agitators, and inciters. If the Jews were still lodged in the body of the German nation, we would probably by now have reached the stage of 1916–17.

The wealth they possessed we took from them. I gave a strict order, which has been carried out by SS Obergruppenführer Pohl, that this wealth will of course be turned over to the Reich in its entirety. We have taken none of it for ourselves. Individuals who have erred will be punished in accordance with the order given by me at the start, threatening that anyone who takes as much as a single Mark of this money is a dead man. A number of SS men – they are not very many – committed this offence, and they shall die. There will be no mercy. We had the moral right, we had the duty towards our people, to destroy this people that wanted to destroy us. But we do not have the right to enrich ourselves by so much as a fur, as a watch, by one Mark or a cigarette or anything else. We do not want, in the end, because we destroyed a bacillus, to be infected by this bacillus and to die. I will never stand by and watch while even a small rotten spot develops or takes hold. Wherever it may form we will together burn it away. All in all, however, we can say that we have carried out this most difficult of tasks in a spirit of love for our people. And we have suffered no harm to our inner being, our soul, our character . . .

Good vs Evil

Elie Wiesel, 'The perils of indifference', 12 April 1999

Born in Sighet in Romania, 'a young Jewish boy from a small town in the Carpathian Mountains', Elie Wiesel grew up speaking Yiddish as a first language and studied Hebrew, but after the area was transferred to Hungary in 1940, the Nazis 'cleansed' the town of its Jews in 1944 – as many as 20,000 – deporting them en masse to concentration camps. On arrival at the Auschwitz-Birkenau camp system, in Poland, Wiesel was separated from his mother and younger sister who were then murdered. He and his father were chosen to undertake slave labour at a nearby rubber-producing plant, where they were starved and beaten. As the Red Army closed in, they were moved to Buchenwald, in Germany, and there Wiesel's father perished from his maltreatment shortly before the camp was liberated by the US Third Army in 1945. Wiesel moved to Paris and worked as a journalist until the French intellectual François Mauriac encouraged him to write his own story which appeared in 1958 as *Night*, becoming the classic work of Holocaust literature. In 1986, he won the Nobel Peace Prize. This beautiful speech, given at the White House before President Bill Clinton, should not be relevant now. But in a new millennium in which new powers race for nuclear weaponry, where new tyrants repress freedoms, where journalists are murdered to snuff out their voices, where anti-Jewish racism thrives on the political left and right, and where brutal nationalisms rail against imagined enemies, read this again. It has never been more timely.

Fifty-four years ago today, a young Jewish boy from a small town in the Carpathian Mountains woke up, not far from Goethe's beloved Weimar, in a place of eternal infamy called Buchenwald. He was finally free, but there was no joy in his heart. He thought there never would be again. Liberated a day earlier by American soldiers, he remembers their rage at what they saw. And even if he lives to be a very old man, he will always be grateful to them for that rage, and also for their compassion.

Though he did not understand their language, their eyes told him what he needed to know – that they, too, would remember, and bear witness.

. . . We are on the threshold of a new century, a new millennium. What will the legacy of this vanishing century be? How will it be remembered in the new millennium? Surely it will be judged, and judged severely, in both moral and metaphysical terms. These failures have cast a dark shadow over humanity: two world wars, countless civil wars, the senseless chain of assassinations (Gandhi, the Kennedys, Martin Luther King, Sadat, Rabin), bloodbaths in Cambodia and Nigeria, India and Pakistan, Ireland and Rwanda, Eritrea and Ethiopia, Sarajevo and Kosovo; the inhumanity in the gulag and the tragedy of Hiroshima. And, on a different level, of course, Auschwitz and Treblinka. So much violence; so much indifference.

What is indifference? Etymologically, the word means 'no difference'.

A strange and unnatural state in which the lines blur between light and darkness, dusk and dawn, crime and punishment, cruelty and compassion, good and evil. What are its courses and inescapable consequences? Is it a philosophy? Is there a philosophy of indifference conceivable? Can one possibly view indifference as a virtue? Is it necessary at times to practise it simply to keep one's sanity, live normally, enjoy a fine meal and a glass of wine, as the world around us experiences harrowing upheavals?

Of course, indifference can be tempting – more than that, seductive. It is so much easier to look away from victims. It is so much easier to avoid such rude interruptions to our work, our dreams, our hopes. It is, after all, awkward, troublesome, to be involved in another person's pain and despair. Yet, for the person who is indifferent, his or her neighbours are of no consequence. And, therefore, their lives are meaningless. Their hidden or even visible anguish is of no interest. Indifference reduces the other to an abstraction.

Over there, behind the black gates of Auschwitz, the most tragic of all prisoners were the Muselmänner, as they were called. Wrapped in their torn blankets, they would sit or lie on the ground, staring vacantly into space, unaware of who or where they were – strangers to their surroundings. They no longer felt pain, hunger, thirst. They feared nothing. They felt nothing. They were dead and did not know it.

Rooted in our tradition, some of us felt that to be abandoned by humanity then was not the ultimate. We felt that to be abandoned by God was worse than to be punished by Him. Better an unjust God than an indifferent one. For us to be ignored by God was a harsher punishment than to be a victim of His anger. Man can live far from God – not outside God. God is wherever we are. Even in suffering? Even in suffering.

In a way, to be indifferent to that suffering is what makes the human being inhuman. Indifference, after all, is more dangerous than anger and hatred. Anger can at times be creative. One writes a great poem, a great symphony. One does something special for the sake of humanity because one is angry at the injustice that one witnesses. But indifference is never creative. Even hatred at times may elicit a response. You fight it. You denounce it. You disarm it.

Indifference elicits no response. Indifference is not a response. Indifference is not a beginning; it is an end. And, therefore, indifference is always the friend of the enemy, for it benefits the aggressor – never his victim, whose pain is magnified when he or she feels forgotten. The political prisoner in his cell, the hungry children, the homeless refugees – not to respond to their plight, not to relieve their solitude by offering them a spark of hope is to exile them from human memory. And in denying their humanity, we betray our own.

Indifference, then, is not only a sin, it is a punishment. And this is one of the most important lessons of this outgoing century's wide-ranging experiments in good and evil.

In the place that I come from, society was composed of three simple categories: the killers, the victims, and the bystanders . . . we felt abandoned, forgotten. All of us did. And our only miserable consolation was that we believed that Auschwitz and Treblinka were closely guarded secrets; that the leaders of the free world did not know what was going on behind those black gates and barbed wire; that they had no

knowledge of the war against the Jews that Hitler's armies and their
accomplices waged as part of the war against the Allies. If they knew, we
thought, surely those leaders would have moved heaven and earth to
intervene. They would have spoken out with great outrage and conviction. They would have bombed the railways leading to Birkenau, just
the railways, just once. And now we knew, we learned, we discovered
that the Pentagon knew, the State Department knew.

. . . The depressing tale of the St Louis is a case in point.[1] Sixty years
ago, its human cargo – nearly 1,000 Jews – was turned back to Nazi
Germany. And that happened after the Kristallnacht, after the first
state-sponsored pogrom, with hundreds of Jewish shops destroyed,
synagogues burned, thousands of people put in concentration camps.
And that ship, which was already in the shores of the United States, was
sent back. I don't understand. Roosevelt was a good man, with a heart.
He understood those who needed help.

Why didn't he allow these refugees to disembark? A thousand
people – in America, the great country, the greatest democracy, the
most generous of all new nations in modern history. What happened?
I don't understand.

Why the indifference, on the highest level, to the suffering of the
victims?

But then, there were human beings who were sensitive to our
tragedy. Those non-Jews, those Christians, that we call the 'Righteous
Gentiles', whose selfless acts of heroism saved the honour of their
faith. Why were they so few? Why was there a greater effort to save
SS murderers after the war than to save their victims during the
war? Why did some of America's largest corporations continue to do
business with Hitler's Germany until 1942? It has been suggested, and
it was documented, that the Wehrmacht could not have conducted its

---

1 The German liner St Louis, carrying Jewish refugees from Germany in 1939, was
denied entry to Cuba, then the United States and Canada. Its passengers were
eventually admitted to Britain, France, Belgium and the Netherlands, and many of
them eventually fell prey to the Nazis.

invasion of France without oil obtained from American sources. How is one to explain their indifference?

And yet, my friends, good things have also happened in this traumatic century: the defeat of Nazism, the collapse of communism, the rebirth of Israel on its ancestral soil, the demise of apartheid, Israel's peace treaty with Egypt, the peace accord in Ireland. And let us remember the meeting, filled with drama and emotion, between Rabin and Arafat that you, Mr President, convened in this very place. I was here and I will never forget it.

And then, of course, the joint decision of the United States and NATO to intervene in Kosovo and save those victims, those refugees, those who were uprooted by a man, whom I believe that because of his crimes, should be charged with crimes against humanity.

But this time, the world was not silent. This time, we do respond. This time, we intervene. Does it mean that we have learned from the past? Does it mean that society has changed? Has the human being become less indifferent and more human? Have we really learned from our experiences? Are we less insensitive to the plight of victims of ethnic cleansing and other forms of injustices in places near and far? Is today's justified intervention in Kosovo, led by you, Mr President, a lasting warning that never again will the deportation, the terrorization of children and their parents, be allowed anywhere in the world? Will it discourage other dictators in other lands to do the same?

What about the children? Oh, we see them on television, we read about them in the papers, and we do so with a broken heart. Their fate is always the most tragic, inevitably. When adults wage war, children perish. We see their faces, their eyes. Do we hear their pleas? Do we feel their pain, their agony? Every minute one of them dies of disease, violence, famine. Some of them – so many of them – could be saved.

And so, once again, I think of the young Jewish boy from the Carpathian Mountains. He has accompanied the old man I have become throughout these years of quest and struggle. And together we walk towards the new millennium, carried by profound fear and extraordinary hope.

Boris Yeltsin, 'We are all guilty', 18 July 1998

The best definition of the horrors of the twentieth century. Boris Yeltsin rose as a Communist Party *apparatchik* to run Sverdlovsk (formerly Yekaterinburg, the city where the last tsar, Nicholas II, and his family were slaughtered by Lenin's Bolsheviks) and then, as a reforming Communist leader, to join the ruling Soviet Politburo under Mikhail Gorbachev. Yeltsin challenged Gorbachev and as the USSR collapsed, he was elected president of Russia. Yeltsin, naturally autocratic but possessing liberal democratic instincts, ended Communist rule, promoted democracy, free press, free speech such as Russia had never seen. Yet simultaneously, he allowed reformers to privatise the economy in a way that enriched the new businessmen and his own family while lawless chaos reigned. When Chechnya tried to seize independence, Yeltsin invaded but the Russian army was humiliated and defeated. Yeltsin himself now resembled an ailing and isolated tsar, often publicly drunk. By 1999, he could no longer go on and with the help of his powerful daughter, he selected a surprising successor named Vladimir Putin.

Yeltsin understood the need to face the crimes of Russian history. He allowed historians to research and expose Stalin's killings and in 1998 he ordered the reburial of the bodies of Nicholas II and his family. At the ceremony he gives this much-neglected, short and simple speech which defines the monstrous ideological crimes of the century of blood.

It is a historic day for Russia. Eighty years have passed since the slaying of the last Russian emperor and his family. We have long been silent about this monstrous crime. We must say the truth: The Yekaterinburg massacre has become one of the most shameful episodes in our history.

By burying the remains of innocent victims, we want to atone for the sins of our ancestors.

Those who committed this crime are as guilty as are those who approved of it for decades. We are all guilty.

It is impossible to lie to ourselves by justifying senseless cruelty on political grounds. The shooting of the Romanov family is a result of an uncompromising split in Russian society into 'us' and 'them'. The results of this split can be seen even now.

The burial of the remains of Yekaterinburg is, first of all, an act of human justice. It's a symbol of unity of the nation, an atonement of common guilt.

We all bear responsibility for the historical memory of the nation. And that's why I could not fail to come here. I must be here as both an individual and the president.

I bow my head before the victims of the merciless slaying.

While building a new Russia, we must rely on its historical experience.

Many glorious pages of Russian history were connected with the Romanovs. But with this name is connected one of the most bitter lessons: Any attempt to change life by violence is condemned to failure.

We must end the century, which has been an age of blood and violence in Russia, with repentance and peace, regardless of political views, ethnic or religious belonging.

This is our historic chance. On the eve of the third millennium, we must do it for the sake of our generation and those to come. Let's remember those innocent victims who have fallen to hatred and violence. May they rest in peace.

Chaim Herzog, 'Hate, ignorance and evil', 10 November 1975

This speech is highly relevant today. In November 1975, the United Nations Resolution 3379 asserted that 'Zionism is a form of racism and racial discrimination', a resolution proposed by Arab countries and backed by the Soviet Union and Soviet satellites, all of them police states and dictatorships. Western democracies and much of South America voted against it but it notoriously passed on a majority vote. The resolution did not stand the test of time: it was revoked by a majority vote in 1991 and is now widely regarded as a racist smear on the history of the UN. At the time, it provoked this eloquent reply by Israel's Ambassador to the United Nations, Chaim Herzog. Born in Ireland, Herzog emigrated to Palestine in the 1930s where his father became chief rabbi. During the Second World War, he served in British military intelligence in Germany (witnessing the concentration camps and helping identify the SS chief Heinrich Himmler before his suicide) then fought in the Arab–Israeli war and worked in Israeli intelligence before later being elected as president.

Mr President.

It is symbolic that this debate, which may well prove to be a turning point in the fortunes of the United Nations and a decisive factor in the possible continued existence of this organization, should take place on November 10. Tonight, thirty-seven years ago, has gone down in history as Kristallnacht, the Night of the Crystals. This was the night in 1938 when Hitler's Nazi stormtroopers launched a coordinated attack on the Jewish community in Germany, burned the synagogues in all its cities and made bonfires in the streets of the Holy Books and the Scrolls of the Holy Law and Bible. It was the night when Jewish homes were attacked and heads of families taken away, many of them never to return. It was the night when the windows of all Jewish businesses and stores were smashed, covering the streets in the cities of Germany with a film of broken glass which dissolved into the millions of crystals which gave that night its name. It was the night which led eventually to the crematoria and the gas chambers, Auschwitz-Birkenau, Dachau, Buchenwald, Theresienstadt and others. It was the night which led to the most terrifying holocaust in the history of man.

... I do not come to this rostrum to defend the moral and historical values of the Jewish people. They speak for themselves. They have given to mankind much of what is great and eternal. They have done for the spirit of man more than can readily be appreciated by a forum such as this one.

I come here to denounce the two great evils which menace society in general and a society of nations in particular. These two evils are hatred and ignorance. These two evils are the motivating force behind the proponents of this resolution and their supporters. These two evils characterize those who would drag this world organization, the ideals of which were first conceived by the prophets of Israel, to the depths to which it has been dragged today.

We are seeing here today but another manifestation of the bitter anti-semitic, anti-Jewish hatred which animates Arab society. Who would have believed that in this year, 1975, the malicious falsehoods of the 'Elders of Zion' would be distributed officially by Arab governments? Who would have believed that we would today contemplate an Arab society which teaches the vilest anti-Jewish hate in the kindergartens? ... We are being attacked by a society which is motivated by the most extreme form of racism known in the world today. This is the racism which was expressed so succinctly in the words of the leader of the PLO [Palestine Liberation Organization], Yasser Arafat, in his opening address at a symposium in Tripoli, Libya: 'There will be no presence in the region other than the Arab presence.' In other words, in the Middle East from the Atlantic Ocean to the Persian Gulf only one presence is allowed, and that is Arab presence. No other people, regardless of how deep are its roots in the region, is to be permitted to enjoy its right to self-determination.

As I stand on this rostrum, the long and proud history of my people unravels itself before my inward eye. I see the oppressors of our people over the ages as they pass one another in evil procession into oblivion. I stand here before you as the representative of a strong and flourishing people which has survived them all and which will survive this shameful exhibition and the proponents of this resolution.

The great moments of Jewish history come to mind as I face you, once again outnumbered and the would-be victim of hate, ignorance and evil. I look back on those great moments. I recall the greatness of a nation which I have the honour to represent in this forum. I am mindful at this moment of the Jewish people throughout the world wherever they may be, be it in freedom or in slavery, whose prayers and thoughts are with me at this moment.

I stand here not as a supplicant. Vote as your moral conscience dictates to you. For the issue is neither Israel nor Zionism. The issue is the continued existence of this organization, which has been dragged to its lowest point of discredit by a coalition of despots and racists.

The vote of each delegation will record in history its country's stand on antisemitic racism and anti-Judaism. You yourselves bear the responsibility for your stand before history, for as such will you be viewed in history. We, the Jewish people, will not forget.

For us, the Jewish people, this is but a passing episode in a rich and event-filled history. We put our trust in our providence, in our faith and beliefs, in our time-hallowed tradition, in our striving for social advance and human values, and in our people wherever they may be. For us, the Jewish people, this resolution based on hatred, falsehood and arrogance, is devoid of any moral or legal value.

Prophets

Moses, 'Thou shall not kill', Exodus 20, Verses 1–26

The most influential speech of all time – probably. Moses's commandments, dictated to him by God as he prayed on Mount Sinai and conveyed by him to the Israelites in the form of tablets of stone, influenced the entire development of Jewish, Christian and Islamic faith and civilisation. Moses – Musa, in Arabic – is mentioned 502 times in the Islamic Koran as both a prophet but also a messenger of God and therefore a precursor of Mohammed himself.

And God spake all these words, saying,

I am the Lord thy God, which have brought thee out of the land of Egypt, out of the house of bondage.

Thou shalt have no other gods before me.

Thou shalt not make unto thee any graven image, or any likeness of any thing that is in heaven above, or that is in the earth beneath, or that is in the water under the earth:

Thou shalt not bow down thyself to them, nor serve them: for I the LORD thy God am a jealous God, visiting the iniquity of the fathers upon the children unto the third and fourth generation of them that hate me;

And shewing mercy unto thousands of them that love me, and keep my commandments.

Thou shalt not take the name of the LORD thy God in vain; for the LORD will not hold him guiltless that taketh his name in vain.

Remember the sabbath day, to keep it holy.

Six days shalt thou labour, and do all thy work:

But the seventh day is the sabbath of the LORD thy God: in it thou shalt not do any work, thou, nor thy son, nor thy daughter, thy manservant, nor thy maidservant, nor thy cattle, nor thy stranger that is within thy gates:

For in six days the LORD made heaven and earth, the sea, and all

that in them is, and rested the seventh day: wherefore the LORD
blessed the sabbath day, and hallowed it.

Honour thy father and thy mother: that thy days may be long upon
the land which the LORD thy God giveth thee.

Thou shalt not kill.

Thou shalt not commit adultery.

Thou shalt not steal.

Thou shalt not bear false witness against thy neighbour.

Thou shalt not covet thy neighbour's house, thou shalt not covet thy
neighbour's wife, nor his manservant, nor his maidservant, nor his
ox, nor his ass, nor any thing that is thy neighbour's.

And all the people saw the thunderings, and the lightnings, and the
noise of the trumpet, and the mountain smoking: and when the
people saw it, they removed, and stood afar off.

And they said unto Moses, Speak thou with us, and we will hear: but
let not God speak with us, lest we die.

And Moses said unto the people, Fear not: for God is come to prove
you, and that his fear may be before your faces, that ye sin not.

And the people stood afar off, and Moses drew near unto the thick
darkness where God was.

And the LORD said unto Moses, Thus thou shalt say unto the children
of Israel, Ye have seen that I have talked with you from heaven.

Ye shall not make with me gods of silver, neither shall ye make unto
you gods of gold.

An altar of earth thou shalt make unto me, and shalt sacrifice
thereon thy burnt offerings, and thy peace offerings, thy sheep,
and thine oxen: in all places where I record my name I will come
unto thee, and I will bless thee.

And if thou wilt make me an altar of stone, thou shalt not build it of
hewn stone: for if thou lift up thy tool upon it, thou hast polluted
it.

Neither shalt thou go up by steps unto mine altar, that thy naked-
ness be not discovered thereon.

Jesus of Nazareth, 'Blessed are the poor in spirit', Sermon on the Mount, St Matthew's Gospel, 1st century AD

Here is probably the most famous speech of all time, given by Jesus of Nazareth to express the essential message of his new teaching. The Sermon appears in the Gospel of Matthew which was probably written around seventy years after his death, much later than Mark's Gospel, the earliest to be written, but it is likely that this collection of sayings is based on a genuine tradition handed down within the Christian movement. Matthew places it early in the ministry of Jesus soon after his baptism when he addressed large crowds in his native region of Galilee.

Matthew 5, Verses 3–11 ('The Beatitudes')
Blessed are the poor in spirit: for theirs is the kingdom of heaven.
  Blessed are they that mourn: for they shall be comforted.
Blessed are the meek: for they shall inherit the earth.
Blessed are they which do hunger and thirst after righteousness: for they shall be filled.
Blessed are the merciful: for they shall obtain mercy. Blessed are the pure in heart: for they shall see God.
Blessed are the peacemakers: for they shall be called the children of God.
Blessed are they which are persecuted for righteousness' sake: for theirs is the kingdom of heaven.
Blessed are ye, when men shall revile you, and persecute you, and shall say all manner of evil against you falsely, for my sake.

Matthew 6, Verses 9–13 ('The Lord's Prayer')
After this manner therefore pray ye:
Our Father which art in heaven, Hallowed be thy name.
Thy kingdom come, Thy will be done in earth, as it is in heaven.

Give us this day our daily bread.

And forgive us our debts, as we forgive our debtors.

And lead us not into temptation, but deliver us from evil: For thine is the kingdom, and the power, and the glory, for ever. Amen.

The Prophet Mohammed, 'Turn then your face towards the Sacred Mosque', from the Surah al-Baqarah ('The Cow'), Verse 2 (144–50), 7th century AD

The holy book of the Koran, together with the sayings of Mohammed, known as the *hadith*, are revered by all Muslims who believe them to be the words of God, expressed through his true prophet. It is hard to exaggerate the influence of every word of the Koran and *hadith* which inspired the spread of Islam during the seventh century, the conquest of a vast Arab empire, and over a thousand years of faith. Today they are studied and learned by millions.

> Indeed we see the turning of your face to heaven, so We shall surely turn you to a qiblah [prayer direction] which you shall like; turn then your face towards the Sacred Mosque, and wherever you are, turn your face towards it, and those who have been given the Book [Scriptures, i.e. Jews and Christians] most surely know that it is the truth from their Lord; and Allah is not at all heedless of what they do.

> And even if you bring to those who have been given the Book every sign they would not follow your qiblah, nor can you be a follower of their qiblah, neither are they the followers of each other's qiblah, and if you follow their desires after the knowledge that has come to you, then you shall most surely be among the unjust.

> Those whom We have given the Book recognize him as they recognize their sons, and a party of them most surely conceal the truth while they know (it).

> The truth is from your Lord, therefore you should not be of the doubters.

> And every one has a direction to which he should turn, therefore hasten to (do) good works; wherever you are, Allah will bring you

all together; surely Allah has power over all things.

And from whatsoever place you come forth, turn your face towards the Sacred Mosque; and surely it is the very truth from your Lord, and Allah is not at all heedless of what you do.

And from whatsoever place you come forth, turn your face towards the Sacred Mosque; and wherever you are turn your faces towards it, so that people shall have no accusation against you, except such of them as are unjust; so do not fear them, and fear Me, that I may complete My favour on you and that you may walk on the right course.

Warnings

J. Robert Oppenheimer, 'We are not only scientists; we are men, too', 2 November 1945

The use of atomic bombs against Japan in 1945 heralded a new era when nuclear warfare could at any moment destroy the entire world. When US President Franklin Roosevelt created the Manhattan Project to develop a powerful new weapon, the scientist Robert Oppenheimer led the Anglo-American team in Los Alamos, New Mexico. On 16 July 1945, the device was tested and in August deployed for the first time against the cities of Hiroshima and Nagasaki. Oppenheimer, who was a leftist scholar with a fascination for Eastern cultures, understood the perils of the new nuclear age: this speech, made to the Association of Los Alamos Scientists, reveals his intellectual rigour and honesty but also his outspoken reservations about American capitalism as well as the perils of nuclear proliferation. After it emerged that many of the Manhattan Project scientists had been Soviet spies who gave the nuclear secrets to Stalin, Oppenheimer was watched by the FBI, suspected of Communist sympathies and lost his security clearance. Over a half a century later, in the twenty-first century, as rogue states such as North Korea and Iran seek nuclear weapons while unstable states such as Pakistan not only have this weaponry but have irresponsibly sold it around the world, the dangers are more urgent than ever.

I should like to talk tonight . . . as a fellow scientist, and at least as a fellow worrier about the fix we are in.

. . . It is not possible to be a scientist unless you believe that it is good to learn. It is not good to be a scientist, and it is not possible, unless you think that it is of the highest value to share your knowledge, to share it with anyone who is interested. It is not possible to be a scientist unless you believe that the knowledge of the world, and the power which this gives, is a thing which is of intrinsic value to humanity, and that you are using it to help in the spread of knowledge, and are willing to take the consequences.

. . . I think it is true to say that atomic weapons are a peril which affect everyone in the world, and in that sense a completely common problem, as common a problem as it was for the Allies to defeat the Nazis. I think that in order to handle this common problem there must be a complete sense of community responsibility . . . the point I want to make, the one point I want to hammer home, is what an enormous change in spirit is involved. There are things which we hold very dear, and I think rightly hold very dear; I would say that the word democracy perhaps stood for some of them as well as any other word. There are many parts of the world in which there is no democracy. There are other things which we hold dear, and which we rightly should. And when I speak of a new spirit in international affairs I mean that even to these deepest of things which we cherish, and for which Americans have been willing to die – and certainly most of us would be willing to die – even in these deepest things, we realize that there is something more profound than that; namely, the common bond with other men everywhere.

. . . We are not only scientists; we are men, too. We cannot forget our dependence on our fellow men . . . These are the strongest bonds in the world, stronger than those even that bind us to one another, these are the deepest bonds – that bind us to our fellow men.

Greta Thunberg, 'We can't solve a crisis without treating it as a crisis', 3 December 2018

A Swedish schoolgirl confronts the world on the crisis that could destroy it. In August 2018, a fifteen-year-old girl walked out of school to spend an afternoon outside the Swedish parliament building to protest about political apathy towards climate change.

By March the following year, Greta Thunberg's campaign had inspired tens of thousands of schoolchildren around the world to go on strike, from countries including the UK, US, Australia, Belgium and Japan. Here is her urgent speech at the UN's COP24 climate change summit.

My name is Greta Thunberg. I am fifteen years old. I am from Sweden. I speak on behalf of Climate Justice Now. Many people say that Sweden is just a small country and it doesn't matter what we do. But I've learned you are never too small to make a difference. And if a few children can get headlines all over the world just by not going to school, then imagine what we could all do together if we really wanted to.

But to do that, we have to speak clearly, no matter how uncomfortable that may be. You only speak of green eternal economic growth because you are too scared of being unpopular. You only talk about moving forward with the same bad ideas that got us into this mess, even when the only sensible thing to do is pull the emergency brake. You are not mature enough to tell it like is. Even that burden you leave to us children. But I don't care about being popular. I care about climate justice and the living planet. Our civilization is being sacrificed for the opportunity of a very small number of people to continue making enormous amounts of money. Our biosphere is being sacrificed so that rich people in countries like mine can live in luxury. It is the sufferings of the many which pay for the luxuries of the few.

The year 2078, I will celebrate my seventy-fifth birthday. If I have children maybe they will spend that day with me. Maybe they will ask me about you. Maybe they will ask why you didn't do anything while there still was time to act. You say you love your children above all else, and yet you are stealing their future in front of their very eyes.

Until you start focusing on what needs to be done rather than what is politically possible, there is no hope. We can't solve a crisis without treating it as a crisis. We need to keep the fossil fuels in the ground, and we need to focus on equity. And if solutions within the system are so impossible to find, maybe we should change the system itself. We have not come here to beg world leaders to care. You have ignored us in the past and you will ignore us again. We have run out of excuses and we are running out of time. We have come here to let you know that change is coming, whether you like it or not. The real power belongs to the people. Thank you.

Goodbyes

Eva Perón, 'Remain faithful to Perón', 17 October 1951

Eva Perón turned her own death into a political and sacred spectacular. Juan Perón, born in 1895, was an Argentine colonel who in 1943 backed a military coup. Eva Duarte was born in 1919 in poverty and illegitimacy in the provinces of the Pampas, moving to Buenos Aires to pursue her career as an actress. When she met Colonel Perón at a gala to raise money for victims of an earthquake he was minister of labour; they fell in love and married. Perón allied himself with the trade unions, fusing nationalism with socialism like the fascist leaders of Europe – and Eva, soon known as Evita, turned out to be a real political asset with an emotional link to the millions of dispossessed workers known as the *descamisados*, 'the shirtless ones'.

When Perón clashed with the generals and was arrested, Evita organised vast demonstrations that led to his release. When Perón was elected president in 1946, Evita ran a foundation to help the poor and dreamed of becoming president herself, travelling around Europe to promote Perón's Argentina. Her glamorous *haute couture* clothes, her jewels, the corruption of her family and the brutality of her henchmen did not offend the *descamisados*, who regarded her rise to be theirs too. Nonetheless, the Peróns were backed by violence and it was no coincidence that Perón, who had openly sympathised with Hitler, gave personal refuge to many of the monstrous killers of the Nazi Holocaust, including Adolf Eichmann, the organiser of the Final Solution, and Josef Mengele, the degenerate doctor who had selected those to die in the gas chambers at Auschwitz and performed sadistic medical experiments on children.

In 1951, Evita announced her candidacy to run for vice-president but her conservative enemies forced her to withdraw. When she became seriously ill with ovarian cancer, Perón arranged for her to be given the title 'Spiritual Leader of the Nation'. Her death in 1952 was greeted with scenes of mass hysteria. Her body was embalmed but plans for a grandiose mausoleum were left unfinished. Perón was mocked for having the thirteen-year-old Nelly Rivas as his mistress at the age of fifty-nine ('I am not superstitious', he joked), and was overthrown in 1955. He fled Argentina and lived in exile. Evita's body was hidden abroad. In 1973, Perón, now almost eighty, returned to power with his third wife Isabel, a former night-club singer. When he died in office, 'Isabelita' succeeded him until she was overthrown by the generals, yet the authority of Perón and the charisma of Evita spawned a Perónist party that has often won elections in Argentina into the twenty-first century.

No speech catches Evita's allure more than this one. Thin and pale, her voice broken, she addresses a million people in October 1951 from the balcony of the Casa Rosada, the presidential mansion. The inspiration behind the song 'Don't Cry for Me Argentina' in the musical *Evita*, the real thing is almost as poignant: and even more ritualistic, plangent and melodramatic. The greatest deathbed performance in history, a masterpiece of pathos.

My beloved descamisados:

Today is a day of many emotions for me. With all my soul I wanted to be with you and Perón on this glorious day of the descamisados. I can't ever miss this October 17 appointment with my people. I assure you that no one or nothing could ever prevent me from coming, because I have a sacred debt to Perón and all of you, to the workers, to the boys of the CGT, to the descamisados and the people. And it doesn't matter to me if I have to leave shreds of my life along the way in order to repay it.

I had to come and I came to give thanks to Perón, to the CGT [trade union federation], to the CGT and the descamisados of my Fatherland.

What I say to Perón, who wanted to honour me with the highest distinction that could be granted a Perónist this evening, is that I will never cease repaying you and would give my life in gratitude for how good you have always been and are with me. Nothing I have, nothing I am, nothing I think is mine: it's Perón's. I will not tell you the usual lies: I won't tell you that I don't deserve this. Yes, I deserve this, my general. I deserve it for one thing alone, which is worth more than all the gold in the world: I deserve it for all I've done for the love of this people. I'm not important because of what I've done; I'm not important because of what I've renounced; I'm not important because of what I am or have. I have only one thing that matters, and I have it in my heart. It sets my soul aflame, it wounds my flesh and burns in my sinews: it's love for this people and for Perón. I gave you thanks, my general, for having taught me to know and love them. If this people asked me for my life I would joyfully give it, for the happiness of one descamisado is worth more than my entire life.

I had to come here to give thanks to the CGT for the homage they pay me in giving me a decoration that in my eyes is the most beloved remembrance of the Argentinian workers. I had to come to thank you for having dedicated this glorious day of the workers and the CGT to this humble woman. And I had to come to tell you that it is necessary, as the general says, to keep the guards on the alert at all the posts of our struggle. The danger has not passed. Every Argentinian worker must keep his eyes open and not fall asleep, for the enemies work in the shade of treason and sometimes are hidden behind a smile or an extended hand. And I had to come to thank all of you, my beloved descamisados from all corners of the Fatherland, for being willing to risk your lives for Perón. I was certain that you knew – as did I – how to serve as Perón's entrenchment. The enemies of the people, of Perón and the Fatherland, have also long known that Perón and Eva Perón are ready to die for this people. Now they also know that the people are ready to die for Perón.

Compañeros, I ask just one thing today: that all of us publicly vow to defend Perón and to fight for him until death. And our oath will be shouted for a minute so that our cry can reach the last corner of the earth: Our lives for Perón!

Let the enemies of the people, of Perón and the Fatherland come. I have never been afraid of them because I have always believed in the people. I have always believed in my beloved descamisados because I have never forgotten that without them October 17 would have been a date of pain and bitterness, for this date was supposed to be one of ignominy and treason, but the courage of this people turned it into a day of glory and happiness. Finally, compañeros, I thank you for all your prayers for my health; I thank you with all my heart. I hope that God hears the humble of my Fatherland so that I can quickly return to the struggle and be able to keep on fighting with Perón for you and with you for Perón until death. I don't ask or want anything for myself. My glory is and always will be to be Perón's shield and the flag of my people, and though I leave shreds of my life along the road, I know that you will pick up my name and will carry it to victory as a banner. I know that God is with us because he is with the humble and despises the arrogance of the oligarchy. This is why victory will be ours. We will achieve it sooner or later, whatever the cost, whoever may fall.

My descamisados: I wanted to tell you many things but the doctors have forbidden me from speaking. I have you in my heart and tell you that it is certain my wish is that I will soon be back in the struggle, with more strength and love, to fight for this people which I love so much, as I love Perón. And I ask you just one thing: it's certain I will soon be with you, but if for health reasons I am not, take care of the general. Remain faithful to Perón as you've been until today, because this means being loyal to the Fatherland and loyal to yourselves. And to all the descamisados of the interior, I hold them closely, so very closely to my heart, and want them to know how much I love them.

Martin Luther King, Jr, 'I've seen the promised land', 3 April 1968

Biblical poetry and fearsome foreboding. Dr Martin Luther King, the preacher and civil rights leader, had already done so much to fight segregation and discrimination since the fifties, delivering the historic Civil Rights Act of 1964 and helping to lead campaigns against Vietnam and now the Poor People's Campaign. In this speech he draws heavily from the Book of Deuteronomy but the implication is dark. Moses led the Israelites all the way from Egypt to the very edge of the Promised Land but he realises his time is limited and he will not see it himself. 'Then Moses climbed Mount Nebo ... There the LORD showed him the whole land ... Then the LORD said to him, "This is the land I promised on oath to Abraham, Isaac and Jacob ... I will let you see it with your eyes, but you will not cross over into it"', reads Deuteronomy 34:1–4. It was four years since the 'I have a dream' speech. But it was a different America: Kennedy had been assassinated, the country was in uproar against the Vietnam war, King was being watched and harassed by the FBI. In Memphis, Tennessee, he talks informally and serenely, mentioning his recovery from a stabbing in 1958 and disdaining long life compared with his dreams. It is a heartbreaking speech and there is no doubt reading it that King sensed imminent danger. It is a goodbye. It was his last night. The next day he was standing on the balcony of the Lorraine Motel when he was assassinated. Others would lead the Israelites into the Promised Land.

You know, several years ago, I was in New York City autographing the first book that I had written. And while sitting there autographing books, a demented black woman came up. The only question I heard from her was, 'Are you Martin Luther King?' And I was looking down writing, and

I said yes. And the next minute I felt something beating on my chest. Before I knew it, I had been stabbed by this demented woman. I was rushed to Harlem Hospital. It was a dark Saturday afternoon. And that blade had gone through, and the X-rays revealed that the tip of the blade was on the edge of my aorta, the main artery. And once that's punctured, you drown in your own blood – that's the end of you.

It came out in the New York Times the next morning that if I had sneezed, I would have died. Well, about four days later, they allowed me, after the operation, after my chest had been opened, and the blade had been taken out, to move around in the wheelchair in the hospital. They allowed me to read some of the mail that came in, and from all over the States, and the world, kind letters came in. I read a few, but one of them I will never forget. I had received one from the president and the vice-president. I've forgotten what those telegrams said. I'd received a visit and a letter from the Governor of New York, but I've forgotten what the letter said. But there was another letter that came from a little girl, a young girl who was a student at the White Plains High School. And I looked at that letter, and I'll never forget it. It said simply, 'Dear Dr King: I am a ninth-grade student at the White Plains High School.' She said, 'While it should not matter, I would like to mention that I am a white girl. I read in the paper of your misfortune, and of your suffering. And I read that if you had sneezed, you would have died. And I'm simply writing you to say that I'm so happy that you didn't sneeze.'

And I want to say tonight, I want to say that I am happy that I didn't sneeze. Because if I had sneezed, I wouldn't have been around here in 1960, when students all over the South started sitting-in at lunch counters. And I knew that as they were sitting in, they were really standing up for the best in the American dream. And taking the whole nation back to those great wells of democracy which were dug deep by the Founding Fathers in the Declaration of Independence and the Constitution. If I had sneezed, I wouldn't have been around in 1962, when negroes in Albany, Georgia, decided to straighten their backs up. And whenever men and women straighten their backs up, they are going somewhere, because a man can't ride your back unless it is bent.

If I had sneezed, I wouldn't have been here in 1963, when the black people of Birmingham, Alabama, aroused the conscience of this nation, and brought into being the Civil Rights Bill. If I had sneezed, I wouldn't have had a chance later that year, in August, to try to tell America about a dream that I had had. If I had sneezed, I wouldn't have been down in Selma, Alabama, to see the great movement there. If I had sneezed, I wouldn't have been in Memphis to see a community rally around those brothers and sisters who are suffering. I'm so happy that I didn't sneeze.

And they were telling me, now it doesn't matter now. It really doesn't matter what happens now. I left Atlanta this morning, and as we got started on the plane, there were six of us, the pilot said over the public address system, 'We are sorry for the delay, but we have Dr Martin Luther King on the plane. And to be sure that all of the bags were checked, and to be sure that nothing would be wrong with the plane, we had to check out everything carefully. And we've had the plane protected and guarded all night.'

And then I got into Memphis. And some began to say that threats, or talk about the threats that were out. What would happen to me from some of our sick white brothers?

Well, I don't know what will happen now. We've got some difficult days ahead. But it doesn't matter with me now. Because I've been to the mountaintop. And I don't mind. Like anybody, I would like to live a long life. Longevity has its place. But I'm not concerned about that now. I just want to do God's will. And He's allowed me to go up to the mountain.

And I've looked over. And I've seen the promised land. I may not get there with you. But I want you to know tonight, that we, as a people will get to the promised land. And I'm happy, tonight. I'm not worried about anything. I'm not fearing any man. Mine eyes have seen the glory of the coming of the Lord.

Attila the Hun, funeral address by his henchman, 'Lord of the bravest tribes fell neither by enemy's blows nor treachery but rejoicing', AD 453

When the most fearsome conqueror in the world dies in his wife's arms on his wedding night, this is how a courtier says goodbye. Attila, King of the Huns, terrorised the eastern and western Roman empires, the very definition of a murderous barbarian. After marrying a new young wife named Ildico, she found him in the morning covered in blood, dead at the height of his power. Recounted by the historian Jordanes quoting Priscus, who had met Atilla, the funeral address celebrates the remarkable fact that after a lifetime of killing and fighting, he died peacefully after a wild night of boozing with a young bride – 'Who can think of this as death?'

Chief of the Huns, King Attila, born of his father Mundzuk, lord of the bravest tribes, who with unprecedented power alone possessed the kingdoms of Scythia and Germany, and having captured their cities terrorised both Roman empires and, that they might save their remnants from plunder, was appeased by their prayers and took an annual tribute. And when he had by good fortune accomplished all this, he fell neither by an enemy's blow nor by treachery, but safe among his own people, happy, rejoicing, without any pain. Who therefore can think of this as death, seeing that no one thinks it calls for vengeance?

Richard Nixon, 'Nobody will ever write a book about my mother', 9 August 1974

The spectacle of a flawed man who has tainted the noble office of president forever – and destroyed himself with the self-inflicted folly of the Watergate scandal. On 8 August 1974, President Nixon announced his resignation on television and the following day his staff, many of them devoted, bewildered and tearful, gather with his family to hear this strange and spontaneous farewell.

I think the record should show that this is one of those spontaneous things that we always arrange whenever the President comes in to speak, and it will be so reported in the press, and we don't mind, because they have to call it as they see it.

But on our part, believe me, it is spontaneous.

You are here to say goodbye to us, and we don't have a good word for it in English – the best is *au revoir*. We'll see you again.

I just met with the members of the White House staff, you know, those who serve here in the White House day in and day out, and I asked them to do what I ask all of you to do to the extent that you can and, of course, are requested to do so: to serve our next President as you have served me and previous Presidents – because many of you have been here for many years – with devotion and dedication, because this office, great as it is, can only be as great as the men and women who work for and with the President.

This house, for example – I was thinking of it as we walked down this hall, and I was comparing it to some of the great houses of the world that I have been in. This isn't the biggest house. Many, and most, in even smaller countries, are much bigger. This isn't the finest house. Many in Europe, particularly, and in China, Asia, have paintings of great, great value, things that we just don't have here and, probably, will never have until we are 1,000 years old or older.

But this is the best house. It is the best house, because it has something far more important than numbers of people who serve, far more important than numbers of rooms or how big it is, far more important than numbers of magnificent pieces of art.

This house has a great heart, and that heart comes from those who serve. I was rather sorry they didn't come down. We said goodbye to them upstairs . . . I recall after so many times I have made speeches, and some of them pretty tough, yet, I always come back, or after a hard day – and my days usually have run rather long – I would always get a lift from them, because I might be a little down but they always smiled.

And so it is with you. I look around here, and I see so many on this staff that, you know, I should have been by your offices and shaken hands, and I would love to have talked to you and found out how to run the world – everybody wants to tell the President what to do, and boy, he needs to be told many times – but I just haven't had the time. But I want you to know that each and every one of you, I know, is indispensable to this Government . . .

Sure, we have done some things wrong in this Administration, and the top man always takes the responsibility, and I have never ducked it.

Mistakes, yes. But for personal gain, never. You did what you believed in. Sometimes right, sometimes wrong. And I only wish that I were a wealthy man – at the present time, I have got to find a way to pay my taxes – and if I were, I would like to recompense you for the sacrifices that all of you have made to serve in government.

But you are getting something in government – and I want you to tell this to your children, and I hope the Nation's children will hear it, too – something in government service that is far more important than money. It is a cause bigger than yourself. It is the cause of making this the greatest nation in the world, the leader of the world, because without our leadership, the world will know nothing but war, possibly starvation or worse, in the years ahead. With our leadership it will know peace, it will know plenty . . .

I remember my old man. I think that they would have called him sort of a little man, common man. He didn't consider himself that way. You know what he was? He was a streetcar motorman first, and then he was a farmer, and then he had a lemon ranch. It was the poorest lemon ranch in California, I can assure you. He sold it before they found oil on it. [Laughter] And then he was a grocer. But he was a great man, because he did his job, and every job counts up to the hilt, regardless of what happens.

Nobody will ever write a book, probably, about my mother. Well, I guess all of you would say this about your mother – my mother was a saint. And I think of her, two boys dying of tuberculosis, nursing four others in order that she could take care of my older brother for three years in Arizona, and seeing each of them die, and when they died, it was like one of her own.

Yes, she will have no books written about her. But she was a saint.

Now, however, we look to the future. I had a little quote in the speech last night from T.R. [Theodore Roosevelt] As you know, I kind of like to read books. I am not educated, but I do read books – and the T.R. quote was a pretty good one. Here is another one I found as I was reading, my last night in the White House, and this quote is about a young man. He was a young lawyer in New York. He had married a beautiful girl, and they had a lovely daughter, and then suddenly she died, and this is what he wrote. This was in his diary.

He said, 'She was beautiful in face and form and lovelier still in spirit. As a flower she grew and as a fair young flower she died. Her life had been always in the sunshine. There had never come to her a single great sorrow. None ever knew her who did not love and revere her for her bright and sunny temper and her saintly unselfishness. Fair, pure and joyous as a maiden, loving, tender and happy as a young wife. When she had just become a mother, when her life seemed to be just begun and when the years seemed so bright before her, then by a strange and terrible fate death came to her. And when my heart's dearest died, the light went from my life forever.'

That was T.R. in his twenties. He thought the light had gone from his life forever – but he went on. And he not only became President but, as an ex-President, he served his country, always in the arena, tempestuous, strong, sometimes wrong, sometimes right, but he was a man.

And as I leave, let me say, that is an example I think all of us should remember. We think sometimes when things happen that don't go the right way; we think that when you don't pass the bar exam the first time – I happened to, but I was just lucky; I mean, my writing was so poor the bar examiner said, 'We have just got to let the guy through.' We think that when someone dear to us dies, we think that when we lose an election, we think that when we suffer a defeat that all is ended. We think, as T.R. said, that the light had left his life forever. Not true.

It is only a beginning, always. The young must know it; the old must know it. It must always sustain us, because the greatness comes not when things go always good for you, but the greatness comes and you are really tested, when you take some knocks, some disappointments, when sadness comes, because only if you have been in the deepest valley can you ever know how magnificent it is to be on the highest mountain.

... Always give your best, never get discouraged, never be petty; always remember, others may hate you, but those who hate you don't win unless you hate them, and then you destroy yourself.

And so, we leave with high hopes, in good spirit, and with deep humility, and with very much gratefulness in our hearts. I can only say to each and every one of you, we come from many faiths, we pray perhaps to different gods – but really the same God in a sense – but I want to say for each and every one of you, not only will we always remember you, not only will we always be grateful to you but always you will be in our hearts and you will be in our prayers.

Thank you very much.

William Pitt the Younger, 'Europe is not to be saved by any single man', 9 November 1805

Modesty and grandeur. These spontaneous words by William Pitt, the British prime minister, are a lesson to any speechmaker, so laconic is their limpid brevity. Pitt was the son of a famous prime minister of the Seven Years' War, William Pitt, Earl of Chatham, hence he was always known as 'the Younger'. He was extraordinarily precocious, becoming chancellor of the exchequer at twenty-one and prime minister at twenty-four. For George III, he was a political saviour after decades of disastrous ministries. But Pitt was soon faced with the recurrences of the king's mysterious mental illness, and then the huge challenge of war against France. Ruling from 1783 to 1801, Pitt was one of Britain's longest-serving premiers. Though he never married, he was extremely gregarious while being socially unambitious and unpretentious, but he gradually became dependent on drinking port: he was nicknamed 'the three-bottle man'. In 1804, he returned to the premiership to face a formidable threat in the ambitions of the new Emperor Napoleon, which he countered by organizing an anti-French coalition with Russia and Austria. In October 1805, Admiral Nelson destroyed the French and Spanish fleets at Trafalgar. At the Lord Mayor's Banquet, Pitt was toasted as 'the Saviour of Europe' to which he responded as follows. His modesty was sensible since Napoleon was about to rout the coalition. When Pitt heard that Russia and Austria had been defeated at the Battle of Austerlitz, he replied calmly, 'Roll up that map; it will not be wanted these ten years.' But he would not live to see it. This speech is a sort of goodbye: he was exhausted and died from a burst ulcer just weeks later.

I return you many thanks for the honour you have done me; but Europe is not to be saved by any single man. England has saved herself by her exertions, and will, as I trust, save Europe by her example.

Nero, 'What an artist the world is losing in me', 9 June 68 AD

Nero was a political performer; his entire life a performance of speeches, poetry recitals, chariot-racing and theatrical displays, played out with the strange and shameless posturing of a camp, preposterous yet sinister exhibitionism. The young Roman emperor merged politics into showbusiness in a way that seems familiar in the twenty-first century. Vainglorious, grandiloquent, self-absorbed and vicious, this melodramatist was theatrical in everything he did.

He was born at the very centre of Roman society and the Julio-Claudian clan that had created the empire, starting with Julius Caesar and then the first emperor Augustus: step-son of his great-uncle Emperor Claudius, son of Agrippina (who was Emperor Caligula's sister) and Gnaeus Domitius Ahenobarbus, Nero was Augustus' great-great-grandson. His formidable mother Agrippina married the ageing, ailing Claudius, whom she persuaded to make Nero joint-heir with his own son by another marriage, the younger Britannicus. She then accelerated the succession by poisoning her husband, ensuring that Nero, aged sixteen, succeeded to the throne. Advised by the brilliant philosopher Seneca, who wrote his first two speeches, Nero soberly praised the late Claudius at his funeral and then addressed the Senate, promising justice and decency.

At first he left government to his advisers and Agrippina, while he studied acting and chariot-racing, but the popularity of Britannicus led him to break the boy's spirit by raping him; and when that did not work, he ordered his poisoning in front of him at a banquet. Nero's mother resented his new independence, so he ordered her murder by shipwreck, but when she survived that, she was stabbed to death. Later he killed his own pregnant wife, kicking her belly. His sexual pleasure-seeking became as

elaborately depraved as his murders. A fratricide, a matricide
and an uxoricide – as well as being generally homicidal, Nero
indulged himself in a reign of both terror and theatre: he performed frequently on stage (the audience was not allowed to
leave during his acts) and as a daredevil charioteer. By 64 AD,
still only in his mid-twenties, he was planning a vast new palace,
the Golden House, decorated with a colossal statue of himself,
when a fire destroyed much of central Rome, with many believing he had started it himself. He blamed it on the Christians
(who were brutally killed in public entertainments) but by now
he was highly unpopular, his rule corrupt and inept. He set out
on a tour of Greece where he gave a famously self-regarding
speech in November 67, preserved in an inscription:

I blame time for squandering the greatness of my gift in advance
   I repay your gods whose concern for me I have constantly experi-
enced both on land and sea
   Other leaders have freed cities but only Nero has freed a province.

But Nero's authority was withering; revolts spread, starting
with the Jews in Jerusalem, and ultimately reaching Rome itself.
His greatest speeches, his ultimate performance, were the lines
(some of them actually from plays in which he had acted) he
loudly declaimed as Rome itself rebelled. It was as if this terrifying, murderous popinjay was so spoilt that he relished any
attention, even playing out the death of an emperor as if it was
a drama. First Nero fled to the port of Ostia, crying out:

Is it so dreadful a thing then to die?

He then practised a speech begging the Senate for mercy, but
back in Rome his very guards deserted him and when he en-
treated someone to kill him and no one offered to do so, he
howled:

Have I neither friend nor foe?

He ran outside and tried to drown himself in the Tiber but then gave up, accompanying his last loyal courtiers to a suburban villa where he ordered the digging of a grave while he prowled up and down, declaiming over and over again:

What an artist the world is losing in me!

When he discovered the Senate planned to beat him to death, he played with two daggers but could not kill himself, now declaring:

To live is a scandal and a shame – this does not become Nero – one should be resolute at such times – come rouse yourself!

As he heard the hooves of the horsemen ordered by the Senate to arrest him alive, he performed another line:

Hark, now strikes on my ear the trampling of swift-footed hunters!

Aided by his secretary, he managed to stab himself in the throat. A horseman tried to stop the bleeding, provoking Nero's last theatrical line:

Too late! So this is loyalty?!

No other leader in history has left the stage with such self-dramatising hysteria as this overpromoted imperial narcissist – the last of the five emperors of the Caesar dynasty.

Barack Obama, 'We do these things because of who we are', 1 May 2011

The hunt for the most wanted man on earth took a decade. Osama bin Laden was the chieftain of the jihadist terror group al-Qaeda, who organized the 9/11 attacks on the Twin Towers in New York and the Pentagon in Washington, DC, using airliners as flying bombs. The attacks were meant to punish America but also to provoke its involvement in the Middle East. In revenge, the Americans invaded first Afghanistan and then Iraq, becoming entangled in asymmetrical wars for over ten years at a vast cost in the lives of US troops and local citizens. Bin Laden was hunted but always managed to escape – until intelligence aircraft discovered that he was living in a villa close to an army base in Pakistan, purportedly a US ally. President Obama gave the order to assassinate bin Laden. His speech announcing the killing is marked by its tightness of phrase and restraint of triumphalism as well as the simple clarity of its statements of America's exceptional sense of self.

Good evening. Tonight, I can report to the American people and to the world that the United States has conducted an operation that killed Osama bin Laden, the leader of al-Qaeda, and a terrorist who was responsible for the murder of thousands of innocent men, women, and children.

It was nearly ten years ago that a bright September day was darkened by the worst attack on the American people in our history. The images of 9/11 are seared into our national memory – hijacked planes cutting through a cloudless September sky; the Twin Towers collapsing to the ground; black smoke billowing up from the Pentagon; the wreckage of Flight 93 in Shanksville, Pennsylvania, where the actions of heroic citizens saved even more heartbreak and destruction.

And yet we know that the worst images are those that were unseen to the world. The empty seat at the dinner table. Children who were forced to grow up without their mother or their father. Parents who would never know the feeling of their child's embrace. Nearly 3,000 citizens taken from us, leaving a gaping hole in our hearts.

On September 11, 2001, in our time of grief, the American people came together. We offered our neighbours a hand, and we offered the wounded our blood. We reaffirmed our ties to each other, and our love of community and country. On that day, no matter where we came from, what God we prayed to, or what race or ethnicity we were, we were united as one American family.

We were also united in our resolve to protect our nation and to bring those who committed this vicious attack to justice. We quickly learned that the 9/11 attacks were carried out by al-Qaeda – an organization headed by Osama bin Laden, which had openly declared war on the United States and was committed to killing innocents in our country and around the globe. And so we went to war against al-Qaeda to protect our citizens, our friends, and our allies.

Over the last ten years, thanks to the tireless and heroic work of our military and our counterterrorism professionals, we've made great strides in that effort. We've disrupted terrorist attacks and strengthened our homeland defense. In Afghanistan, we removed the Taliban government, which had given bin Laden and al-Qaeda safe haven and support. And around the globe, we worked with our friends and allies to capture or kill scores of al-Qaeda terrorists, including several who were a part of the 9/11 plot.

Yet Osama bin Laden avoided capture and escaped across the Afghan border into Pakistan. Meanwhile, al-Qaeda continued to operate from along that border and operate through its affiliates across the world.

And so shortly after taking office, I directed Leon Panetta, the director of the CIA, to make the killing or capture of Bin Laden the top priority of our war against al-Qaeda, even as we continued our broader efforts to disrupt, dismantle, and defeat his network.

Then, last August, after years of painstaking work by our intelligence community, I was briefed on a possible lead to Bin Laden. It was far from certain, and it took many months to run this thread to ground. I met repeatedly with my national security team as we developed more information about the possibility that we had located Bin Laden hiding within a compound deep inside of Pakistan. And finally, last week, I determined that we had enough intelligence to take action, and authorized an operation to get Osama bin Laden and bring him to justice.

Today, at my direction, the United States launched a targeted operation against that compound in Abbottabad, Pakistan. A small team of Americans carried out the operation with extraordinary courage and capability. No Americans were harmed. They took care to avoid civilian casualties. After a firefight, they killed Osama bin Laden and took custody of his body . . .

As we do, we must also reaffirm that the United States is not – and never will be – at war with Islam . . .

The American people did not choose this fight. It came to our shores, and started with the senseless slaughter of our citizens. After nearly ten years of service, struggle, and sacrifice, we know well the costs of war. These efforts weigh on me every time I, as Commander-in-Chief, have to sign a letter to a family that has lost a loved one, or look into the eyes of a service member who's been gravely wounded.

So Americans understand the costs of war. Yet as a country, we will never tolerate our security being threatened, nor stand idly by when our people have been killed. We will be relentless in defense of our citizens and our friends and allies. We will be true to the values that make us who we are. And on nights like this one, we can say to those families who have lost loved ones to al-Qaeda's terror: Justice has been done.

Tonight, we give thanks to the countless intelligence and counterterrorism professionals who've worked tirelessly to achieve this outcome. The American people do not see their work, nor know their names. But tonight, they feel the satisfaction of their work and the result of their pursuit of justice.

We give thanks for the men who carried out this operation, for they exemplify the professionalism, patriotism, and unparalleled courage of those who serve our country. And they are part of a generation that has borne the heaviest share of the burden since that September day.

Finally, let me say to the families who lost loved ones on 9/11 that we have never forgotten your loss, nor wavered in our commitment to see that we do whatever it takes to prevent another attack on our shores.

And tonight, let us think back to the sense of unity that prevailed on 9/11. I know that it has, at times, frayed. Yet today's achievement is a testament to the greatness of our country and the determination of the American people.

The cause of securing our country is not complete. But tonight, we are once again reminded that America can do whatever we set our mind to. That is the story of our history, whether it's the pursuit of prosperity for our people, or the struggle for equality for all our citizens; our commitment to stand up for our values abroad, and our sacrifices to make the world a safer place.

Let us remember that we can do these things not just because of wealth or power, but because of who we are: one nation, under God, indivisible, with liberty and justice for all.

Thank you. May God bless you. And may God bless the United States of America.

Napoleon Bonaparte, 'Soldiers of my Old Guard: I bid you farewell', 20 April 1814

In April 1814, Napoleon Bonaparte, the former Emperor of the French who had previously ruled much of Europe, addressed the devoted veterans of his Old (or Imperial) Guard in the courtyard at the palace of Fontainebleau before leaving to go into exile on the small island of Elba. While it is estimated that over 2 million had died in wars mainly launched to aggrandise his own rule, his very short speech to his Guard is a sublime performance by a maestro of political theatre. By turns dramatic, self-pitying, paternalistically emotional and delusional, his shameless claims that he had ruled, conquered and abdicated for the sake of France work beautifully on the grizzled veterans who sob at his words. The hint that he has allowed himself to survive only to save France and his veterans is preposterously self-serving too but it reveals that he had attempted suicide a few days earlier, taking an opium overdose that he survived after a night of vomiting. It was an astonishing career – and it was not yet over. Soon he would be back for a last throw of the iron dice.

Soldiers of my old Guard, I bid you farewell. For twenty years you have been my constant companions on the road to honour and glory. In these latter times, as in the days of our prosperity, you have never ceased to be models of courage and fidelity. With men such as you our cause would not have been lost; but the war would have been interminable; it would have been a civil war, and France would only have become unhappier still. I have therefore sacrificed all of our interests to those of the nation; I shall depart. But you, my friends, continue to serve France. Her happiness was my only thought; it shall continue to be the object of my desires. Do not lament my fate; the only reason I have allowed myself to survive was so that I could further serve our glory. I want to write down the great deeds which we have done together. Adieu, my children! Would that I could press you all to my heart. Let me at least embrace your standard!

Once again, adieu, my old companions! May this last kiss pass to your hearts!

Edward VIII, 'The woman I love', 11 December 1936

Love and renunciation – the definition of passionate romance and of shallow egotism. The entire British empire listened to this radio speech by the King-Emperor Edward VIII who, given the choice of reigning as the British monarch or marrying his paramour, the American Wallis Simpson, chose love. Her status as a divorcee – which would nowadays seem trivial – was then regarded as unacceptable for a king's wife. While his listeners were dazzled by the sheer romance of his sacrifice, his narcissistic and unwise personality were soon revealed during his visits to Hitler, secret flirtations with Nazi collaboration, aimless life and ultimately long and discontented marriage to Wallis. Perhaps Britain was lucky to lose its lovestruck king. His successor was his stammering brother George VI, who proved a selfless servant like his daughter Elizabeth II.

At long last I am able to say a few words of my own. I have never wanted to withhold anything, but until now it has not been constitutionally possible for me to speak.

A few hours ago I discharged my last duty as King and Emperor, and now that I have been succeeded by my brother, the Duke of York, my first words must be to declare my allegiance to him. This I do with all my heart.

You all know the reasons which have impelled me to renounce the throne. But I want you to understand that in making up my mind I did not forget the country or the empire, which, as Prince of Wales and lately as King, I have for twenty-five years tried to serve.

But you must believe me when I tell you that I have found it impossible to carry the heavy burden of responsibility and to discharge my duties as King as I would wish to do without the help and support of the woman I love.

And I want you to know that the decision I have made has been mine and mine alone. This was a thing I had to judge entirely for myself. The other person most nearly concerned has tried up to the last to persuade me to take a different course.

I have made this, the most serious decision of my life, only upon the single thought of what would, in the end, be best for all.

This decision has been made less difficult to me by the sure knowledge that my brother, with his long training in the public affairs of this country and with his fine qualities, will be able to take my place forthwith without interruption or injury to the life and progress of the empire. And he has one matchless blessing, enjoyed by so many of you, and not bestowed on me – a happy home with his wife and children.

And now, we all have a new King. I wish him and you, his people, happiness and prosperity with all my heart. God bless you all! God save the King!

Alexander the Great, 'Depart!', August 324 BC

Alexander the Great was defeated once – by the mutiny of his own soldiers. This is the bitter, angry and exasperated speech of the greatest conqueror of all time faced with the disloyalty of his own generals and troops. Inheriting the throne of Macedonia as a teenager, Alexander conquered the Persian empire, Central Asia, Afghanistan and then invaded India. He faced the challenge of ruling his empire with just a few Macedonians and so he needed to include local Persian governors too. Crafting a merged Persian and Macedonian empire ruled from Babylon, he wanted to conquer the world as a living god but his Macedonian soldiers, while devoted to their king, feared his ambitions and his tyranny, and the favour he showed to his new Persian subjects. His Indian expedition was a step too far. His mutinous troops forced him to stop and he returned to Babylonia by ship. On return, he executed generals who opposed him and, no doubt infuriated by his obstinate troops, he promoted Persian officers. Then he announced at Opis that he would pay off the debts of his oldest veterans and send them back to Macedonia. Convinced that he was replacing them with Persians, they mutinied. Alexander subjected them to this withering speech, reminding them what they had achieved together, starting from his father Philip II.

Then he sulked in his tent. Shamed, his men buckled and begged for forgiveness. They went but Alexander's troubles intensified. On his way back to Babylon, his only trusted henchman and sometime lover, Hephaistion, died, possibly of poison. Alexander was heartbroken and surrounded by conspiracies. He arranged a mass marriage of Macedonian soldiers and Persian girls. Back in Babylon, Alexander planned a new campaign to conquer Arabia but after another drinking bout, he died on 10/11 June 323 BC aged thirty-two. This speech, as recorded by the later historian Arrian, is his best, astonishing in its wounded pride, divine fury, heroic vision and terrifying contempt. Of course the claim that he did it all for his people, always the excuse of the world conqueror, is ultimately empty: he wished to be the ruler of the world for its own sake.

The speech which I am about to deliver will not be for the purpose of checking your start homeward, for, so far as I am concerned, you may depart wherever you wish; but for the purpose of making you under-stand when you take yourselves off, what kind of men you have been to us who have conferred such benefits upon you.

In the first place, as is reasonable, I shall begin my speech from my father Philip. For he found you vagabonds and destitute of means, most of you clad in hides, feeding a few sheep up the mountain sides, for the protection of which you had to fight with small success against Illyrians, Triballians, and the border Thracians. Instead of the hides he gave you cloaks to wear, and from the mountains he led you down into the plains, and made you capable of fighting the neighbouring barbarians, so that you were no longer compelled to preserve yourselves by trusting rather to the inaccessible strongholds than to your own valour. He made you colonists of cities, which he adorned with useful laws and customs; and from being slaves and subjects, he made you rulers over those very barbarians by whom you yourselves, as well as your property, were previously liable to be carried off or ravaged. He also added the greater part of Thrace to Macedonia, and by seizing the most conveniently situated places on the sea-coast, he spread abundance over the land from commerce, and made the working of the mines a secure employment. He made you rulers over the Thessalians, of whom you had formerly been in mortal fear; and by humbling the nation of the Phocians, he rendered the avenue into Greece broad and easy for you, instead of being narrow and difficult. The Athenians and Thebans, who were always lying in wait to attack Macedonia, he humbled to such a degree, I also then rendering him my personal aid in the campaign, that instead of paying tribute to the former and being vassals to the latter, those states in their turn procure security to themselves by our assistance.

He penetrated into the Peloponnese, and after regulating its affairs, was publicly declared commander-in-chief of all the rest of Greece in the expedition against the Persian, adding this glory not more to himself than to the commonwealth of the Macedonians. These were the advantages which accrued to you from my father Philip; great indeed if looked at by themselves, but small if compared with those you have obtained from me. For though I inherited from my father only a few gold and silver goblets, and there were not even sixty talents in the treasury . . . I started from the country which could not decently support you, and forthwith laid open to you the passage of the Hellespont, though at that time the Persians held the sovereignty of the sea. Having overpowered the satraps of Darius with my cavalry, I added to your empire the whole of Ionia, the whole of Aeolis, both Phrygias and Lydia, and I took Miletus by siege. All the other places I gained by voluntary surrender, and I granted you the privilege of appropriating the wealth found in them.

The riches of Egypt and Cyrene, which I acquired without fighting a battle, have come to you. Coele-Syria, Palestine, and Mesopotamia are your property. Babylon, Bactra, and Susa are yours. The wealth of the Lydians, the treasures of the Persians, and the riches of the Indians are yours; and so is the External Sea. You are viceroys, you are generals, you are captains. What then have I reserved to myself after all these labours, except this purple robe and this diadem? I have appropriated nothing myself, nor can any one point out my treasures, except these possessions of yours or the things which I am guarding on your behalf. Individually, however, I have no motive to guard them, since I feed on the same fare as you do, and I take only the same amount of sleep. Nay, I do not think that my fare is as good as that of those among you who live luxuriously; and I know that I often sit up at night to watch for you, that you may be able to sleep.

But someone may say, that while you endured toil and fatigue, I have acquired these things as your leader without myself sharing the toil and fatigue. But who is there of you who knows that he has endured greater toil for me than I have for him? Come now, whoever of you has wounds, let him strip and show them, and I will show mine in turn; for there is no part of my body, in front at any rate, remaining free from wounds; nor is there any kind of weapon used either for close combat or for hurling at the enemy, the traces of which I do not bear on my person. For I have been wounded with the sword in close fight, I have been shot with arrows, and I have been struck with missiles projected from engines of war; and though oftentimes I have been hit with stones and bolts of wood for the sake of your lives, your glory, and your wealth, I am still leading you as conquerors over all the land and sea, all rivers, mountains, and plains. I have celebrated your weddings with my own, and the children of many of you will be akin to my children. Moreover I have liquidated the debts of all those who had incurred them, without inquiring too closely for what purpose they were contracted, though you received such high pay, and carry off so much booty whenever there is booty to be got after a siege. Most of you have golden crowns, the eternal memorials of your valour and of the honour you receive from me. Whoever has been killed has met with a glorious end and has been honoured with a splendid burial. Brazen statues of most of the slain have been erected at home, and their parents are held in honour, being released from all public service and from taxation. But no one of you has ever been killed in flight under my leadership. And now I was intending to send back those of you who are unfit for service, objects of envy to those at home; but since you all wish to depart, depart all of you!

Go back and report at home that your king Alexander, the conqueror of the Persians, Medes, Bactrians, and Sacians; the man who has subjugated the Uxians, Arachotians, and Drangians; who has also acquired the rule of the Parthians, Chorasmians, and Hyrcanians, as far as the Caspian Sea; who has marched over the Caucasus, through the Caspian Gates; who has crossed the rivers Oxus and Tanais, and the Indus besides, which has never been crossed by anyone else except Dionysus; who has also crossed the Hydaspes, Acesines, and Hydraotes, and who would have crossed the Hyphasis, if you had not shrunk back with alarm; who has penetrated into the Great Sea by both the mouths of the Indus; who has marched through the desert of Gadrosia, where no one ever before marched with an army; who on his route acquired possession of Carmania and the land of the Oritians, in addition to his other conquests, his fleet having in the meantime already sailed round the coast of the sea which extends from India to Persia – report that when you returned to Susa you deserted him and went away, handing him over to the protection of conquered foreigners. Perhaps this report of yours will be both glorious to you in the eyes of men and devout I ween in the eyes of the gods. Depart!

Charles I, 'I go from a corruptible to an incorruptible crown', 30 January 1649

Charles I was not meant to succeed his father James I. The eldest son was the much-loved Henry Prince of Wales, named after the glorious Tudor Henrys while Charles was tiny, shy and sickly. But Henry died young and Charles became the heir. An early incident suggested a lack of political and personal judgement: in 1623, enthralled by romantic chivalry, he and his father's favourite the Duke of Buckingham embarked on a secret mission, travelling incognito across Europe to woo the Spanish Infanta – without having negotiated how to reconcile her Catholicism and the staunch Protestantism of the English. His father the king was horrified when the two young men returned empty-handed. Charles later made a happy marriage, a love match, to Henrietta Maria, daughter of the King of France. On his succession, he kept Buckingham as effective chief minister but the flamboyant Lord High Admiral bungled an English military expedition against Spain and was already under Parliamentary attack when he was assassinated.

Unable to work with Parliament, the king ruled alone from 1629, funding himself with ingenious taxes that gradually infuriated the gentry while simultaneously enforcing his own vision of high Protestantism through his overbearing Archbishop Laud which led to rebellion in Scotland. Convinced of his own rectitude in all matters as a divine king, Charles was proud, brave, touchy, inflexible and unwise but also ruthless and duplicitous in his own actions. At the same time, he was a loving husband and father and a munificent patron of the arts. Forced to recall Parliament in 1640, he then had to sacrifice his chief minister the Earl of Strafford who was beheaded, but to no avail. Within two years, the king was raising his standard in a civil war against his own Parliament with the ruling class divided between the two. After losing battles, he was captured by Parliament but while negotiating, he escaped, leading to more bloodshed. By the time he was recaptured, the Parliamentary leader, Oliver Cromwell, regarded the king as 'the author of our troubles' and many saw him as 'the man of blood'. In late 1648, Cromwell and the army purged Parliament which permitted the unthinkable: the king was placed on trial. Charles refused to recognise the court or case but after ten days he was found guilty of high treason and other crimes. Cromwell particularly agonised over the execution but he and fifty-nine others – the regicides – signed his death sentence. A scaffold was built outside the Banqueting Hall of Whitehall in London.

On 30 January 1649, Charles, wearing two shirts so that he would not appear to shiver in the cold, is led out and addresses the crowd.

I shall be very little heard of anybody here . . . Indeed, I could hold my peace very well, if I did not think that holding my peace would make some men think that I did submit to the guilt, as well as to the punishment: but I think it is my duty to God first, and to my country, for to clear myself both as an honest man, and a good King and a good Christian.

I shall begin first with my innocency. In troth I think it not very needful for me to insist upon this, for all the world knows that I never did begin a war with the two Houses of Parliament, and I call God to witness, to whom I must shortly make an account, that I never did intend for to incroach upon their privileges, they began upon me, it is the militia they began upon, they confess that the militia was mine, but they thought it fit for to have it from me.

God forbid that I should be so ill a Christian, as not to say that God's judgements are just upon me: many times he does pay justice by an unjust sentence, that is ordinary: I will only say this, that an unjust sentence that I suffered to take effect, is punished now by an unjust sentence upon me, that is, so far I have said, to show you that I am an innocent man.

Now for to show you that I am a good Christian: I hope there is a good man that will bear me witness, that I have forgiven all the world, and even those in particular that have been the chief causers of my death: who they are, God knows, I do not desire to know, I pray God forgive them.

But this is not all, my charity must go farther, I wish that they may repent, for indeed they have committed a great sin in that particular: I pray God with St Stephen, that this be not laid to their charge, nay, not only so, but that they may take the right way to the peace of the kingdom, for my charity commands me not only to forgive particular men, but my charity commands me to endeavour to the last gasp the peace of the kingdom . . .

. . . For the people: and truly I desire their liberty and freedom as much as any body whomsoever, but I must tell you, that their liberty and their freedom consists in having of government; those laws, by which their life and their goods may be most their own.

It is not for having share in government (Sirs) that is nothing pertaining to them; a subject and a sovereign are clean different things, and therefore until they do that, I mean, that you do put the people in that liberty as I say, certainly they will never enjoy themselves. Sirs, it was for this that now I am come here: if I would have given way to an arbitrary way, for to have all laws changed according to the power of the sword, I needed not to have come here, and therefore I tell you (and I pray God it be not laid to your charge) that I am the martyr of the people.

In troth Sirs, I shall not hold you much longer, for I will only say thus to you, that in truth I could have desired some little time longer, because I would have put then that I have said in a little more order, and a little better digested than I have done, and therefore I hope you will excuse me.

I have delivered my conscience, I pray God that you do take those courses that are best for the good of the kingdom, and your own salvations.

. . . In troth Sirs, my conscience in religion I think is very well known to all the world, and therefore I declare before you all, that I die a Christian, according to the profession of the Church of England, as I found it left me by my father, and this honest man I think will witness it.

. . . I have a good cause, and a gracious God on my side . . . I go from a corruptible to an incorruptible crown; where no disturbance can be, no disturbance in the world.

Ronald Reagan, 'Nothing ends here; our hopes and our journeys continue', 28 January 1986

The seven astronauts on the Space Shuttle *Challenger* summed up America: five men, two women, five white, one African-American and one Asian-American – one was a schoolteacher. The launch was set for 28 January 1986. At 11:39, the NASA shuttle orbiter was launched and 73 seconds into its rocket-propelled flight, it exploded and disintegrated, killing all seven instantly. President Reagan is due to give his State of the Union address but it is clear immediately that he has to give a different sort of speech. He turns to his best speechwriter, Peggy Noonan, a New Yorker and former CBS writer with a beautiful turn of phrase that she is able to adapt to Reagan's folksy yet theatrical oratory. After the *Challenger* explosion, she uses the words of poet John Magee about aviators who 'slipped the surly bonds of earth . . . and touched the face of God' to create one of the most admired speeches in the twentieth century.

Ladies and Gentlemen, I'd planned to speak to you tonight to report on the state of the Union, but the events of earlier today have led me to change those plans. Today is a day for mourning and remembering. Nancy and I are pained to the core by the tragedy of the shuttle *Challenger*. We know we share this pain with all of the people of our country. This is truly a national loss.

Nineteen years ago, almost to the day, we lost three astronauts in a terrible accident on the ground. But we've never lost an astronaut in flight. We've never had a tragedy like this.

And perhaps we've forgotten the courage it took for the crew of the shuttle. But they, the *Challenger* Seven, were aware of the dangers, but overcame them and did their jobs brilliantly. We mourn seven heroes: Michael Smith, Dick Scobee, Judith Resnik, Ronald McNair, Ellison Onizuka, Gregory Jarvis, and Christa McAuliffe.

We mourn their loss as a nation together.

For the families of the seven, we cannot bear, as you do, the full impact of this tragedy. But we feel the loss, and we're thinking about you so very much. Your loved ones were daring and brave, and they had that special grace, that special spirit that says, 'Give me a challenge, and I'll meet it with joy.' They had a hunger to explore the universe and discover its truths. They wished to serve, and they did. They served all of us.

We've grown used to wonders in this century. It's hard to dazzle us. But for twenty-five years the United States space program has been doing just that. We've grown used to the idea of space, and, perhaps we forget that we've only just begun. We're still pioneers. They, the members of the Challenger crew, were pioneers.

And I want to say something to the schoolchildren of America who were watching the live coverage of the shuttle's take-off. I know it's hard to understand, but sometimes painful things like this happen. It's all part of the process of exploration and discovery. It's all part of taking a chance and expanding man's horizons. The future doesn't belong to the faint-hearted; it belongs to the brave. The Challenger crew was pulling us into the future, and we'll continue to follow them.

I've always had great faith in and respect for our space program. And what happened today does nothing to diminish it. We don't hide our space program. We don't keep secrets and cover things up. We do it all up front and in public. That's the way freedom is, and we wouldn't change it for a minute.

We'll continue our quest in space. There will be more shuttle flights and more shuttle crews and, yes, more volunteers, more civilians, more teachers in space. Nothing ends here; our hopes and our journeys continue.

I want to add that I wish I could talk to every man and woman who works for NASA, or who worked on this mission and tell them: 'Your dedication and professionalism have moved and impressed us for decades. And we know of your anguish. We share it.'

There's a coincidence today. On this day three hundred and ninety years ago, the great explorer Sir Francis Drake died aboard ship off the coast of Panama. In his lifetime the great frontiers were the oceans, and an historian later said, 'He lived by the sea, died on it, and was buried in it.' Well, today, we can say of the Challenger crew: their dedication was, like Drake's, complete.

The crew of the Space Shuttle Challenger honored us by the manner in which they lived their lives. We will never forget them, nor the last time we saw them, this morning, as they prepared for their journey and waved goodbye and 'slipped the surly bonds of earth' to 'touch the face of God.'

Written in History

Letters that Changed the World

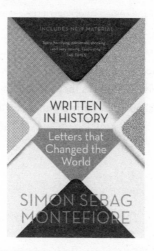

A collection of the greatest letters in history, charting world-shaping events and revealing the unique personalities of some of history's most famous figures

Acclaimed historian Simon Sebag Montefiore selects over one hundred letters from ancient times to the twenty-first century: some are noble and inspiring, some despicable and unsettling; some are exquisite works of literature, others brutal, coarse and frankly outrageous. The writers vary from Elizabeth I, Rameses the Great and Leonard Cohen to Emmeline Pankhurst, Mandela and Stalin – from love letters to calls for liberation, declarations of war to reflections on death. In the accessible style of a master storyteller, Montefiore shows why these letters are essential reading: how they enlighten our past, enrich the way we live now – and illuminate tomorrow.

The Romanovs

1613–1918

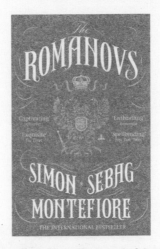

The internationally bestselling epic history of Russia's imperial dynasty

The Romanovs were the most successful dynasty of modern times, ruling a sixth of the world's surface. How did one family turn a war-ruined principality into the world's greatest empire? And how did they lose it all? This is the intimate story of twenty tsars and tsarinas, some touched by genius, some by madness, but all inspired by holy autocracy and imperial ambition. Drawing on new archival research, *The Romanovs* is at once an enthralling chronicle of triumph and tragedy, love and death, a universal study of power, and an essential portrait of the empire that still defines Russia today.

Jerusalem

The Biography

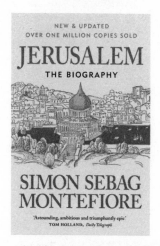

The epic story of Jerusalem told through the lives of the men and women who created, ruled and inhabited it

Jerusalem is the universal city, the capital of two peoples, the shrine of three faiths; it is the site of Judgement Day and the battlefield of today's clash of civilisations. How did this small, remote town become the Holy City, the 'centre of the world' and now the key to peace in the Middle East? Drawing on new archives and a lifetime's study, Simon Sebag Montefiore reveals this ever-changing city through the wars, love affairs and revelations of the men and women – kings, empresses, prophets, poets, saints, conquerors and whores – who created, destroyed, chronicled and believed in Jerusalem.

Young Stalin

What makes a Stalin? Was he a Tsarist agent or Lenin's bandit? Was he to blame for his wife's death? When did the killing start?

Based on revelatory research, here is the thrilling story of how a charismatic cobbler's son became a student priest, romantic poet, prolific lover, gangster mastermind and murderous revolutionary. Culminating in the 1917 revolution, Simon Sebag Montefiore's bestselling biography radically alters our understanding of the gifted politician and fanatical Marxist who shaped the Soviet empire in his own brutal image. This is the story of how Stalin became Stalin.

Stalin

The Court of the Red Tsar

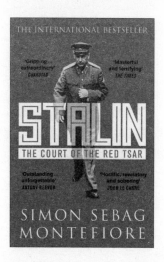

A thrilling biography of Stalin and his entourage during the terrifying decades of his supreme power

Stalin: The Court of the Red Tsar has become a classic of modern history writing, transforming our understanding of Stalin as Soviet dictator, Marxist leader and Russian tsar. Based on ground-breaking research, Simon Sebag Montefiore reveals in captivating detail the fear and betrayal, privilege and debauchery, family life and murderous cruelty of this secret world. *Stalin* is an intimate portrait of a man as complicated and human as he was brutal and chilling.

Catherine the Great and Potemkin

The Imperial Love Affair

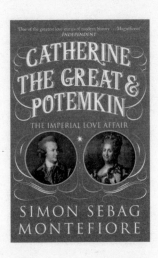

The epic bestselling biography of Catherine the Great and Prince Potemkin, her outrageous lover and co-ruler

It was history's most successful political partnership – as sensual and fiery as it was creative and visionary. Catherine the Great was a woman of notorious passion and imperial ambition. Prince Potemkin was wildly flamboyant and sublimely talented. Together they seized Ukraine and Crimea, defining the Russian empire to this day. Drawing on their intimate letters and on vast research, Simon Sebag Montefiore's enthralling, widely acclaimed biography restores these imperial partners to their rightful place as titans of their age.